MUCH ADO

A SUMMER WITH A REPERTORY THEATER COMPANY

MICHAEL LENEHAN

MIDWAY

AN AGATE IMPRINT

CHICAGO

Printed in the United States

Costume drawings on pages 14, 22, 38, and 84 courtesy
Robert Morgan and American Players Theatre.

Much Ado
ISBN-13: 978-1-57284-205-2
ISBN-10: 1-57284-205-9
First printing: October 2016

Library of Congress Cataloging-in-Publication Data
has been applied for.

10 9 8 7 6 5 4 3 2 1   16 17 18 19 20

Midway is an imprint of Agate Publishing. Agate books are
available in bulk at discount prices.

agatepublishing.com

To Mary, who brought me here

CAST OF CHARACTERS

―――――

AMERICAN PLAYERS THEATRE
SPRING GREEN, WISCONSIN

Much Ado About Nothing, summer 2014

LEONATO – Governor of Messina, played by Brian Mani

HERO – Leonato's virginal daughter, played by Kelsey Brennan

BEATRICE – Leonato's orphaned niece, an unmarried woman, played by Colleen Madden

DON PEDRO – Prince of Aragon, and a matchmaker, played by Jeb Burris

BENEDICK – a lord and soldier in Don Pedro's army, well acquainted with Beatrice, played by David Daniel

CLAUDIO – a young lord and soldier, smitten by Hero, played by Nate Burger

DON JOHN – Pedro's bastard brother, the villain, played by Eric Parks

BORACHIO, CONRAD – followers of Don John, played by Marcus Truschinski and Christopher Sheard

MARGARET — a gentlewoman attendant on Hero, friendly with Borachio, played by Cristina Panfilio

URSULA — another gentlewoman in Leonato's household, played by Abbey Siegworth

ANTONIO — Leonato's older brother, played by Paul Bentzen

FRIAR FRANCIS — a priest, played by John Taylor Phillips

BALTHASAR — a musician in the retinue of Don Pedro, played by Robert Doyle

OTHERS including Dogberry, constable of Messina, and his associate Verges, played by James Pickering and Tim Gittings; a sexton, a messenger, the men of the Watch, and musicians, guests, and attendants played by Jake Penner, Chris Klopatek, Cordell Cole, Robert Doyle, Hendrix Gullixson, Victoria Nassif, and Anne E. Thompson

—

DIRECTOR — David Frank

STAGE MANAGER — Evelyn Matten

COSTUME AND SET DESIGNER — Robert Morgan

COMPOSER AND SOUND DESIGNER — John Tanner

CHOREOGRAPHER — Linda Fortunato

COSTUME DIRECTOR — Scott Rött

DRAPER — April McKinnis

WIGMAKERS — Becky Scott, Lara Dalbey, Maria Davis

TECHNICAL DIRECTOR — Bill Duwell

A NOTE ABOUT THE TEXT

American Players Theatre (APT) prepared a spiral-bound script of the play for internal use, based on the text of the Arden edition published by Bloomsbury. In this book I quote from *The Norton Shakespeare*, which differs from APT's version slightly, mostly in matters of punctuation.

The Norton text uses square brackets [like these] to indicate stage directions inserted by editors after the publication of the First Folio (1623, seven years after Shakespeare's death). Where I quote the play, I have followed the Norton's use of brackets, and used parentheses (like this) to indicate my own interjections and clarifications. In interviews and other quoted material, however, I follow the convention of using square brackets to distinguish my words from the speaker's.

In a few speeches I have cut words and lines that might puzzle readers or lead them away from the point I was trying to make. These edits are indicated by ellipses . . . a device that Shakespeare does not appear to have used.

In school they teach you that collaboration is everybody doing the same thing. It's not true. Nobody's doing the same thing. We all have different things in our heads. What we're doing is coordinating those things, constantly, so the final product is coherent. It's not one idea, it's hundreds of ideas that somehow come into alignment. Everyone's picking up something from somebody else and using it or adjusting to it. And it's just so much fun! Nobody ever really knows how it's going to turn out. And so the excitement is, OK, we're doing this, it's feeling right, it's making sense. But is it going to be any good? Is it going to make sense later on? Sometimes it does, sometimes it doesn't.

—COSTUME AND SET DESIGNER ROBERT MORGAN

needed; something is happening. They exit stage left as Hero and Beatrice descend the stairs from the bridge. Almost immediately Leonato is back, followed by a messenger in military uniform. Leonato holds a sheet of paper in his hand and reads from it. "I learn in this letter that Don Pedro of Aragon comes this night to Messina." Thus begins American Players Theatre's 2014 production of *Much Ado About Nothing*.

David Frank, the director, choreographs from the fourth row. He stands on the balls of his feet, arms stretched out before him, thumbs touching forefingers. He rotates his right wrist so his palm faces upward. He beckons Hero forward by drawing his hand in toward his chest. He waves in the servant, pushes Leonato across the stage to his exit, then waves them back with the messenger and a few more members of the household. He lowers a hand to bring down the music and cues Leonato to speak.

Except there is no Leonato, no actors at all, no costumes, no lights, no audience but a few staffers scattered through the outdoor theater. The only people onstage are the props crew, who are patiently applying plastic foliage to a metal fence on the set. Up in the thirteenth row, at a table sheltered from the sun by beach umbrellas, composer John Tanner and sound technician John Leahy are huddled over a MacBook Pro, setting volume levels for the opening music and sound cues. Leahy taps a key and the music rolls over the empty seats and out into the woods. Frank requests an adjustment and the music plays again. And again, while Frank waves up the imaginary lights and conducts the timing of his invisible actors. He can see it all in his head. He has two more weeks to get it onstage where 1,100 paying customers can see it too.

Will he be able to stifle the "most famous laugh line in the play"? Will his lead actor succeed in his first big romantic role? Will Frank's relationship with the set designer, a longtime friend and collaborator, survive to see another play? Will the critics like the show? Will the audience come? Will the weather cooperate? How many pairs of pants will the leading man ruin? On this sunny afternoon in June, all remains to be seen.

The work began about ten months ago, in late summer of 2013. By the time the theater's outdoor season ends on October 5, the show will have been performed 27 times for a potential audience of about 31,000 people. It will involve a cast of 22 actors playing 27 roles, plus an artistic and production staff of 7, including a choreographer, a composer-sound designer, a costume and set designer, a lighting designer, and a voice and text coach. It will require 46 costumes, 14 wigs, and a wardrobe staff to clean, repair, and restyle the costumes and wigs as necessary for each performance. The show will be played on a multilevel set made almost entirely by carpenters and craftsmen in the company's employ. It will have to support the weight and antics of the actors and yet come apart in little more than half an hour, and fold up into a storage space the size of a small bedroom. The theater's staff numbers about 200 people at the height of the season. As they learn the lines and sew the dresses and make the wigs and build the set for this production, they will do the same for four other plays: *Romeo and Juliet*, Oscar Wilde's *The Importance of Being Earnest*, David Mamet's *American Buffalo,* and Joan Didion's *The Year of Magical Thinking*. And when those shows are up and running, they will mount three more. By mid-August they will have eight plays in rotation, and in October they'll cap the season with a ninth.

Like the man said: much ado.

PLAY IN THE WOODS

———

Back in the days when whimsy was thought to be a desirable quality for internet addresses, APT's website was *playinthewoods.org*. The woods, and trekking through them from the parking lot to the "Up the Hill" stage, have always been an important part of the company's identity. And despite its unlikely location just south of Spring Green, Wisconsin, population 1,628, APT ranks among the country's elite classical theater companies, with an annual budget of about $6 million and ticket sales of more than 100,000 each season.

The company was founded in 1979 by a small group of big thinkers led by Randall Duk Kim, a highly regarded classical actor who wanted a stage far from the coasts, which he found "too frantic" for the kind of theater he wanted to do. Kim had played

Hamlet at the Guthrie Theatre in Minneapolis and had toured with the company in a production of Gogol's *Marriage*. He was impressed by the way midwesterners listened. Near Spring Green, a rural community with an arty bent—it's the home of Frank Lloyd Wright's Taliesin and the associated school of architecture—Kim and his colleagues found a natural amphitheater with excellent acoustics, and there in 1980 they presented their first season of two plays: *A Midsummer Night's Dream* and (lest anyone get the idea that this company would be pandering to popular taste) one of Shakespeare's least performed and most vilified works, *Titus Andronicus*, which one local critic promptly dubbed "a Renaissance *Texas Chainsaw Massacre*."

Kim and his companions—they were Chuck Bright and James "Dusty" Priebe, whom Kim had met at the University of Hawaii, and Anne Occhiogrosso, who joined them after they came to the mainland in 1970—were hardcore idealists: artists and visionaries, not promoters. Marketing was not a high priority for them; they wanted their work to sell itself. In their first year one journalist complained that he couldn't find the theater for lack of road signs. The audience found it anyway. Kim, an extraordinary actor and a master of makeup, could play Shylock one night, Hamlet the next, and carry the whole company on the strength of his talent. He insisted on performing Shakespeare's plays exactly as published in the Folio of 1623, the closest thing we have to a definitive edition of Shakespeare's works. There were no cuts, no changes, no concessions to audience sensibilities. He also insisted that the actors research every word of the text, so the unfamiliar language could be made clear to modern audiences.

It worked—up to a point. The company quickly established a reputation for uncompromising yet entertaining shows, and slowly the audience grew. But the founders' vision encompassed more. They believed that the level of performance they aspired to required a training academy, a library, a center for classical theater research—an institution, in other words, that could not flourish without major financial support. The big money never came and the company couldn't get ahead of its expenses. Twelve years into the dream the audience was still using portable toilets.

The founders moved on after the 1991 season. To replace them the board hired as artistic director David Frank, a 47-year-old Englishman who had worked at regional theaters in Baltimore, Saint Louis, and Buffalo. Frank was a rare find, a dedicated artist who could balance a budget. Together with his business-side counterpart Sheldon Wilner, who had been managing director of APT since 1988, he continued the artistic trajectory of the company and set it on firm financial ground as well. APT finally installed permanent bathrooms in 1995, established a core company of actors in 1999, retired its debt in 2003, and added a 200-seat indoor theater in 2009.

It took longer than the founders expected—and more compromises, probably, than they would have stood for—but today the company they established bears at least a passing resemblance to the one they envisioned, with apprentice and education programs, a resident company of actors, and a text-first approach to the classics. Back in the beginning Kim told a reporter, "I don't say we will be the best theater in the country right from the start, but from the start we are aiming there." In 2014, the *Wall Street Journal*'s drama critic, Terry Teachout, called APT "the best classical theater company in America."

By that time Frank's production of *Much Ado About Nothing* was up and running. He was set to retire at the end of the season, having announced some years before (perhaps a tad prematurely, he later admitted) that 70 would be an appropriate age for him to go. Though he would remain in Spring Green and continue to mount shows as a visiting director, *Much Ado* was the last Shakespeare he would direct as head of the company.

it is uncharacteristically realistic for a Shakespeare comedy. There are no twins, no shipwreck, no cross-dressing, no magic, and only small, contrived cases of mistaken identity. In lieu of these tropes we get a couple of dumb young lovers; an older couple, more worldly and wordy, whose antagonistic wise-cracking no doubt inspired the screwball comedies of the 30s and 40s; and, for low comic effect, the bumbling bumpkins of the Watch, who anticipate the Keystone Kops of the silent movies.

We also get a lot of nothing. The title, which may seem a casual, self-deprecating joke, could in fact be a richly layered pun. According to the Harvard scholar Marjorie Garber, "nothing" was Shakespearean slang for the feminine sex parts (a woman has "no thing"), of which much ado is certainly made in this play. Besides that, and perhaps more to the point, Garber and others believe that the Elizabethan pronunciation of "nothing" was likely the same as "noting," as in taking note or observing. "Note this before my notes," says the self-effacing musician Balthasar before playing a note. "There's not a note of mine that's worth the noting." In *Much Ado* the characters are constantly noting each other, and often misinterpreting what they note. In particular, they overhear things they are not meant to hear and believe they're overhearing things they are meant to hear. And some of them are just lying. Complications ensue.

As the play opens, Don Pedro, prince of Aragon, has just prevailed in some kind of military action, having lost only a few men, and those of the expendable sort—"none of name." The details of this war are not important; all we need to know is that a number of strapping young men, their testosterone elevated by the thrill of battle, are about to descend on the household of Leonato, governor of the Sicilian province of Messina. Of course Leonato has a beautiful young daughter, and a beautiful but sharp-tongued niece, and assorted beautiful gentlewomen-in-waiting. He also has sense enough of his place in the social order to know that he's obliged to feed and entertain the prince's whole retinue, and pretend to like it, for as long as they choose to stay.

Included in this band of randy brothers are Claudio, a young soldier who has distinguished himself in battle and promptly falls in love with Leonato's daughter, Hero; his older buddy Benedick, who has apparently been here before and had some sort of relationship with Leonato's fiery niece, Beatrice, with whom he conducts a "merry war" of wit; and Don John, Don Pedro's bastard brother, a brooding fellow who seems to have opposed the prince in the recent fighting. Or maybe not, Shakespeare doesn't really say. In any case he is now "reconciled" with his brother—but not really, of course, for his envy and villainy are needed to set the plot in motion.

Don Pedro, worldly wise prince and commander,

seems to have something of a Cupid complex. He offers to woo Hero on callow Claudio's behalf. But as they hatch this scheme, their conversation is overheard by a servant. The news gets mangled in the retelling, and Leonato is led to believe that the prince himself wants to marry his daughter—a match that would repay the governor nicely for his forced hospitality. Meanwhile another servant, a sidekick of the bastard Don John, overhears the same news but without the mangling. Seeing an opportunity to make trouble, Don John persuades Claudio to believe, as Leonato does, that the prince is wooing Hero for himself. Claudio's heart is thus twice broken: he thinks that Hero is lost and that his comrade Don Pedro has betrayed him.

But this is merely preliminary trouble and it's quickly cleared up. Don Pedro wins Hero for Claudio as promised. Leonato happily agrees to the match, though it's less than he'd hoped for, and the day of the wedding is set. The prince, made merry by his matchmaking prowess, now moves on to a bigger challenge. If Leonato, Claudio, and Hero will help him, he will "undertake one of Hercules' labors": induce the bickering Beatrice and Benedick to fall in love with each other.

That's enough to get us started. We're at the end of act 2, scene 1, roughly a quarter of the way through the play. Of course the bastard has more tricks up his sleeve. And so does the playwright.

BEATRICE

═══

In late summer 2013, when David Frank knew for sure he would be directing *Much Ado*, he didn't have to think about who would be his Beatrice: Colleen Madden would. She is one of the company's stars, a small woman with a big voice, an extraordinary actress. I saw her take Benedick's arm in playful surrender to their newly blossomed love, and moments later I watched enraptured as he knelt before her and asked, "How doth your cousin?"

"Very ill," Beatrice replies.

"And how do you?"

She looks deep into his eyes; all the protective cynicism has melted from her face, transformed into trust and devotion. Her hand goes to her breast. "Very—ill—too."

I bought it completely. She loved this guy so much she could barely stand it.

And then I saw her do it again, and again, and again, dozens of times over the course of the summer, every time as utterly convincing as the first. That's acting, I suppose, but Madden's ability to conjure that quiet emotion and reproduce it precisely night after night was a revelation to me.

"I have very clear memories since the third and fourth grade of doing school plays, and I really loved it," Madden told me. "That lit my fire. But I never considered doing it for a living. It just didn't occur to me. I assumed I'd be a teacher like my parents." Her mother was an Irish immigrant, her father the grandson of Irish immigrants. When they met, in New York, she was thinking about going back to Ireland and he was on his way out of the priesthood. He was a Franciscan and a peace and justice activist. He later became a psychology professor, she a special-ed teacher, but the two of them were always "very active on the social justice scene," Madden remembered.

The family moved around some and eventually settled in Pittsburgh. Madden studied Chinese at the University of Pittsburgh and along the way spent about two and a half years in China and Taiwan. "I loved studying the writing, and I loved speaking it, but I didn't really love living there. So when it became time to apply for grad school, my heart really wasn't in it. I remember I went to a play in Pittsburgh and saw a director I had worked with—I had been doing plays all through college, in the community or in college productions, and I was getting a fair amount of notice—so during intermission of this play I saw this director and he said, so, I'm assuming you're going to grad school for theater. And it hit me like a thunderbolt that I could do this—this was a possibility!"

She wound up at the University of Delaware's Professional Theatre Training Program, a three-year classical program founded by Sanford (Sandy) Robbins, who had transplanted it to Delaware from the Milwaukee campus of the University of Wisconsin. While in Milwaukee Robbins and his program had developed strong ties to APT, and the relationship continued after they moved east.

"That's where I met David Frank," Madden recalled. "He came, as I think he had for every class, because APT used a lot of students from the program. He saw a play that I happened to be in, and then the next year I graduated and I auditioned for him in New York. And he didn't take me that year, because I was Equity. I had been offered a union job as soon as I got out of grad school. And I remember I auditioned for him, and he was very very nice, but he was saying, well, we're trying to save money to re-cover the seats. He was saying we can't afford another union person. OK, whatever, but of course I figured he's just not into me."

Evidently, and not for the last time, she was failing to grasp Frank's intention. "A year later I get a call out of the blue from Brenda DeVita, whom I'd never met." DeVita was APT's casting director at the time; she has now succeeded Frank as artistic director. "She said, we're looking for someone to play Sonya in *Uncle Vanya*. I know I've never met you but David loves your work. Can I offer you a contract?"

It was January 2001. By this time Madden had appeared in an off-Broadway show and played a doctor on ABC's *All My Children*. There was some talk of a long-term role there. She was "cater-waitering" as a hedge against leaner times, but she had a good deal on a nice apartment in Brooklyn and on the whole was pleased with her New York situation, and wary of leaving it. "I'd always heard about APT, and I was interested in going. But when I first got the call from Brenda, it was a bit of a hard sell. It's the actor's plight: Should I take this job? Even some of my friends now who are doing well in TV and film—they still go: Should I, shouldn't I? That's part of the reason we have agents, people making those decisions for us."

New York agents tend to take a dim view of places like APT. It's *where*? They want you for *how long*? Madden's agent was reluctant. But in 2001, SAG and AFTRA, the TV, film, and radio actors' unions, were threatening to strike. If they did, not much would be happening in New York. "I didn't want to go for six months, but there was probably going to be a strike. I was probably safe. Some friends said no! You've got to stay. You're getting a lot of work. Some said oh no, you should go; you've always wanted to go to APT. And one of my friends said I think you're going to go to APT, you're going to love it, you're going to meet a guy there, and you're going to get married.

"That sounded terrible."

But she took a flyer. "And at the airport I met another actor from New York, who also was getting some traction in his career. He was also coming to APT; we found each other at the gate. He said the strike surely is going to happen, I think we're safe. After we got to APT, we got news that the strike was not happening. He was unhappy. He did not have a good time that year. He was just full of regret and didn't fit in.

"And I was just full of joy. And just had a marvelous time. I loved it immediately. I took to the company, they took to me, I loved the difficult conditions—the bats and the mosquitoes and the hot and the cold and the rain—and I loved having to walk up the hill for rehearsals."

As predicted, she met a guy—an actor, James Ridge. On their first date, she rode with him on his motorcycle. At the end of the season, both were invited to join APT's "core company," which meant a long-term commitment and a guaranteed wage.

They got married. They bought a house and had kids. It's a life that not many actors get to live. Now Madden's mother lives nearby (her father is deceased) and her brother Aran has come from Pittsburgh to found Furthermore Beer, Spring Green's microbrew. Madden is active in the community and something of a celebrity in a very small town.

"Some of the people I worked with, the folks who came to New York to make it big, they thought I was crazy. I remember having a discussion with one of my friends whom I'd just done the off-Broadway show with. She was saying oh my gosh, you don't want to go to Wisconsin; you'll miss everything here. But as far as I know, she's not acting anymore. It's hard to stay acting in New York, to make a living and do things that are actually satisfying to the soul.

"I did worry that I might be missing out on something, and I certainly have. But that's life. You open a door and other doors close. If I had stayed in New York and somehow become very famous, I don't think that life would have suited me at all. I like this kind of work. It has afforded me a family. We're not making buckets of money, but it's OK, and I have room to breathe.

"As soon as I got to Spring Green, I felt at home. I remember looking up that night and seeing the stars—I hadn't seen the stars in like a year."

BENEDICK

—————

Though David Frank knew from the outset who would play Beatrice, he had no idea who would play her opposite, Benedick. He had a few possibilities in mind, but none of them was David Daniel.

Daniel was practically born into the theater. His father and mother met as teenagers at a Massachusetts theater company that took in troubled kids. It was run by a Methodist minister named Dick Waters, who became Daniel's godfather and the first of several mentors he mentions in tracing his career.

Waters called his troupe the Fisherman's Players of Cape Cod—a nod to the area's commercial heritage, surely, but mostly a reference to the Fisher of Men. "This was social-political theater," Daniel told me. "It was the mid-60s. We did plays that dealt with man's place in society, man's obligation to man, the kind of thing that afterward people would go to the coffeehouse for wine and cheese and they'd argue about the play."

Daniel had his first role at age three and a half. "I got to suck my thumb and drag a dead weasel across the stage. My dad played my brother and my mom played my mom."

By the time Daniel was school age the family was living in Virginia, where Daniel's father had grown up. He ran a dinner theater there and stayed active in the business well into the 80s. Young David was not much of a student; when he finished high school the army seemed like a good idea. That's where he fell in love with Shakespeare.

He was stationed in Germany, guarding the border between the Communists and the free world even as the wall in Berlin came down. "The army had this great program with the University of Maryland where you could go away to do a course. So if I wanted to study art, I could go to the Louvre; if I wanted to study Shakespeare, I could go to Stratford-upon-Avon. How could you say no to this? So I saved up some of my leave and I flew to England and stayed at Stratford-upon-Avon for a week and studied Shakespeare. Got to see the Royal Shakespeare Company and the Globe and a whole bunch of plays. For a whole week that's all we did, study the plays, write papers. It was a

MUCH ADO

"BENEDICK"

college credit. That's when I decided I really, really wanted to do this.

"What made it possible is, I went out after the shows and the guy who played Macbeth was in the pub, drinking. It was the same thing as the Shed [the Spring Green tavern where APT people hang out]. And I was astounded that one of *those guys* would be in the bar. And he bought me a drink and he sat down and talked with me, and I was just, oh my God! It wasn't that some actor was talking to me, because I had been raised by actors. I knew actors. This *Shakespeare* actor was talking to me. And I realized that Shakespeare wasn't quite what I thought it was. I remember thinking, I can do this! This guy is a normal, regular guy. He just clocked out. That's his job. He rolled up his sleeves and he just put his head down and did it. I can do that. I'm a worker. So that's when I decided that this is the theater that I wanted to do."

Back in the states, out of the army, he broke the news to his father, who was dismayed but could hardly complain. He attended Virginia Commonwealth University for a few semesters before he ran out of money, then found some work doing roles with the theater departments at women's colleges. He devised an ingenious plan to drive down to Orlando and audition at Disney World—"That was the extent of the plan right there. Just get in the car, get some money for gas, knock on the Disney

World door"—but on the way, in Greenville, South Carolina, he wandered into a theater, just looking for a show, and found his second mentor, Jack Young, who's now head of actor training at the University of Houston and artistic director of the Houston Shakespeare Festival. "He was standing on a ladder, hanging lights." Daniel asked if there would be a play tonight. Young asked if Daniel was an actor. They fell into conversation. "He had a lot of really great questions for me. Like what do you want to do? How will you go about doing it? I told him about my master plan, going down to Disney. He said that sounds like a terrible plan. He said I'm starting this journeyman program, I've got a bunch of young actors like yourself who are looking for big roles, and I've got a theater that I need to cast shows in. I said that sounds kind of interesting. And it was six years I ended up staying there."

Daniel became "bigger and stronger and better" in Young's journeyman program, until "one day Jack pulled me aside and said, you're really good, but at this point you're kind of loud, and you can chew scenery. You need some craft; you need somebody who's really going to hone that down." What he needed was grad school. But he had no undergraduate degree. Young pointed him toward Sandy Robbins, mentor number three, whose program at Delaware was one of the few in the country that would admit a student solely on the strength of an audition.

At Delaware Daniel met mentor number four, David Frank. "He came to audition us; he's this English man doing Shakespeare, and we're in a Shakespeare school, and so everything he said was gospel. We were immediately drawn to him. Not just because of his British accent but because of this blazing white hair, and the guy is so charming and wonderful, and you can't understand half of what he says. He'd stop midsentence: 'You see, you know?' *No, I don't see. Yes, yes, I want to know!* He was so passionate about Shakespeare—not just Shakespeare but the power of poetic language. Everyone in that class just wanted to be closer to him and understand him."

Daniel also met his wife at Delaware—Paula Hubman, an actress. After graduating from the program they took acting jobs here and there, including Beatrice and Benedick at Theatre Aspen in Colorado, while Daniel tried to get through the door at APT. It took a couple years but finally he landed his first role there in 2000, as Demetrius in *A Midsummer Night's Dream.* He and Paula moved to Spring Green and they've been there ever since. They have three sons. In the off-season Daniel works as APT's education director, giving workshops on Shakespeare and poetry to school kids throughout Wisconsin. The example of his mentors seems to animate him. Often after a performance you'll find him with a group of adolescents who follow him eagerly down the hill, flushed and chattering as though they'd just seen a rock show and met one of the guys in the band.

—

When casting began for the 2014 production of *Much Ado*, "DD," as everyone at APT calls him, was beginning his fifteenth season there. He was a member of the core company and had recently done well in a critically acclaimed production of *The Cure at Troy*. But that had been a short-run show in the company's small indoor theater; not many people had seen it. Daniel was not among the company's best-known actors and he had never played a romantic lead. He's a good soldier who claims to enjoy and learn from whatever roles he gets—often the ones he calls the lordies or dukies. It is not like him to ask for a big part. But he wanted Benedick.

He had played the role twice before coming to APT and had tried for it the last time they did the play, in 2007. (He got the friar.) Evelyn Matten, the stage manager of the 2014 production, a friend and fellow Delaware grad, told him he would make a great Benedick and urged him to go for it. So despite his reticence, and despite having been told by the higher-ups that he wasn't being considered for the part, he asked if he could read for it. "They were like, yeah, OK, if you don't mind auditioning.

Not many core people audition, because they're core—they don't need to audition anymore. I love auditioning. And so I go in there and I audition, and David Frank says, 'Well, that's kind of interesting. . . . Oh! I never thought of that before. . . . Let's bring Colleen in.'"

In the play, according to Don Pedro's matchmaking plot, Benedick and Beatrice are induced to fall in love—or to realize that they have always been in love—in two consecutive "gulling" scenes. (The verb is *to gull*, as in gullible.) In the first, Benedick hides in an orchard, thinking he's eavesdropping, while Don Pedro, Claudio, and Leonato histrionically discuss Beatrice's ardent love for him—which they are fabricating on the spot. They are sad for Beatrice, they say, for if Benedick were to learn of her love "He would make but a sport of it and torment the poor lady worse." Claudio says he hears all this from Hero, his betrothed, who is privy to her cousin's misery: "Then down upon her knees she falls, weeps, sobs, beats her heart, tears her hair, prays, curses, 'O sweet Benedick! God give me patience.'" Leonato agrees: "She doth indeed, my daughter says so, and the ecstasy hath so much overborne her that my daughter is sometime afeard she will do a desperate outrage to herself."

In APT's version, Leonato now pauses a beat to make sure Benedick is taking it in. Then: "It is very true."

When the prince and his accomplices finish their performance and walk off, Benedick emerges from his hiding place and gives a soliloquy:

> This can be no trick. The conference was sadly borne. They have the truth of this from Hero. They seem to pity the lady. It seems her affections have their full bent. Love me! Why, it must be requited.

This was one of the speeches that Daniel did in his audition.

"It was funny," Frank remembered. "I just threw in something, just instinctively. I said, 'Do something for me. Would you keep her face in your mind the whole time you're doing the speech? Because you really do just adore her.' And he turned around and it was totally different! It was different from how I've ever heard it, and it was different from how I'd ever imagined it. His heart was on his sleeve—way out."

Daniel repunctuated one of Shakespeare's lines, from "Love me! Why, it must be requited" to "Love me? Why? It must be requited!" He was not the first actor to change the "why" from an interjection to a question. Kenneth Branagh did it ("to great comedic effect," Daniel told me) in his 1993 film version, and no doubt hundreds if not thousands of actors have done the same. What Frank had never heard before, Daniel said, was his reading of

"Love me?," which turned his "why" into plaintive puzzlement.

One possible reading of Beatrice and Benedick is that they are parallel characters, male and female versions of the same witty cynic, both transformed by their friends' deceptions and the resulting emergence of their own deeply buried feelings. The gulling scene and the speech that follows could be played light, strictly for laughs. But Daniel's reading produced something else: an aging stud who has outgrown the military life of male banter and serial womanizing; a wounded soldier who's begun to fear that his chance for romance and satisfying companionship is slipping away.

"He had given his heart to Beatrice before and it didn't work out," Daniel told me. "His monologue is not for laughs, it is absolutely: Is this true, does she really love me? I'm hiding and I'm listening. Not oh, I'm stuck in a bush and I'm peeking my head out. No, it was, I'm lost in my life. I'm lost. And here's a woman who loves me. In the audition, I think everyone's expectations were set on a different track and it took everyone off guard— including myself. *Oh my God, look, he's really hurt inside!* And all it took was that line to get it. 'Love me?' That's the moment where it clicked for me, and I think that's exactly the moment that David's talking about as well."

As Frank remembered it, Carey Cannon, the

associate artistic director, a former actress, was in the room at the time. "I remember turning to Carey: Oh! And I said, give me a minute, David, and I think I went back into the room after that and said, would you do it? It was that decisive."

THE SET

Robert Morgan, the costume and set designer for *Much Ado*, started talking with David Frank about it when all of 2013's shows were up and running. He had never seen a live production of the play, but he had seen filmed versions, and he knew that at minimum the set would require two hiding places, one for each of the gulling scenes. These scenes are not only crucial to the plot, they also provide the play's best opportunity for what the theater people call "lazzi" (LOT-see), by which they mean broad and usually physical comedic business. It's the plural form of the Italian word *lazzo*, or joke, commonly used in connection with commedia dell'arte.

Lazzi sells. As the only Shakespeare comedy on APT's 2014 schedule, *Much Ado* was to be the cash cow of the season. At an average ticket price of $36, its 27 scheduled performances represented potential sales of about $1.1 million. (*Romeo and Juliet* and *The Importance of Being Earnest* were next in line with 24 and 23 performances respectively.) But Frank did not want to rely on the play's easy laughs. He told Morgan he also wanted something a little darker and more substantial.

Frank and Morgan have been working together for more than 30 years, since Frank was artistic director of the Studio Arena Theatre in Buffalo, New York. They are close friends and Morgan, who lives in Vermont, is such a fixture at APT that he owns a small house near Spring Green.

They decided to set the play in Italy, as Shakespeare had, but to move the period up to the mid-19th century. That's where this play often lands, Frank told me: close enough to our time that the costumes and sets won't look too strange, but distant enough to allow for the peculiar social strictures that circumscribe the characters' lives. Frank was thinking mostly about the females. The social world of the play is an oppressive patriarchy. Lest it be overlooked, Shakespeare offers this song of advice for the women:

> Sigh no more, ladies, sigh no more,
> Men were deceivers ever;
> One foot in sea, and one on shore,
> To one thing constant never.

Then sigh not so, but let them go,
And be you blithe and bonny,
Converting all your sounds of woe
Into *Hey, nonny nonny.*

"We talked in the beginning about the male dominance of the society," Morgan recalled. "David kept talking about big stone walls. He wanted a sense of rooted, stone Messina—old, kind of semi-ruined; permanence, structure. I don't remember if he used the word dangerous, but there was clearly a dark undertone that he was responding to and that he wanted in the set. He didn't want summer, he didn't want pretty flowers, he didn't want romance. He wanted all those things that represented the male part of the play. Because he was feeling that was at the core of Hero's experience, and Beatrice is clearly at odds with it."

Working at home in Vermont, Morgan designed a set that in his mind reflected that social order: an outdoor space, maybe a garden, with several vertical elements, a lion's head fountain (referring to the patriarch, Leonato), and two curving staircases flanked by two rows of trees, which would serve as the hiding places. He made it as a scale model of cardboard and wood, about the size of a hatbox. "I wish I had a picture of it," he told me, "but I was so upset I just threw the whole thing in the trash.

"I flew out with it in September and showed it

to David. I was very excited, because I had never seen a set like this on that stage. And he looked at it and said, oh, no no no no no no." Too symmetrical, Frank said, too orderly. He wanted tension, a hint of chaos.

Morgan cut the set down to one staircase and one row of trees, but then Michael Broh, the company's production manager, said even the one curving staircase was too expensive to build.

Agitated now, Morgan replaced the curved staircase with a dogleg and wound up with a set that he thought was very efficient and functional, but devoid of meaning: "A totally generic piece of work, it's not specific to this play at all. You could do *Twelfth Night* on it, you could do *Love's Labour's Lost*, you could do *Taming of the Shrew* on it. It's sort of faceless and doesn't tell you anything."

Frank seemed to love it. During the seven weeks of rehearsal, he carried Morgan's scale model almost everywhere and referred to it constantly. The disorder he wanted to see was realized in an alcove-like space in the back, a rock-walled hollow enclosed by a wrought-iron fence. Morgan had added it as a second hiding place when he eliminated the row of trees stage right. In Frank's mind it was a dark and dirty place. It's been there forever but no one's gone in for a long, long time. The gate is rusty and difficult to open and the chamber behind it is gnarly, dank, overgrown—corrupt.

Whether the set was generic or expressive, Frank and Morgan agreed that above all it functioned well as a theatrical space. "I think all the spaces work really well," Morgan said. "It gives David the spaces he needs to stage the play." He pointed out the semicircular bridge, the raised area toward the back of the stage; an actor could stand three feet back from its edge, he said, and still be seen from every seat in the house. He pointed to the staircase, which gave the actors two places to stand that were elevated above the main floor. He pointed to the floor, a "stone" patio that defined and focused the space and also provided a periphery that the actors could step down onto. "That provides a good tension for people," he said.

As he went on it became clear that a big part of his job, as he saw it, was to give the actors spaces to act in. Morgan didn't know it when he designed the set, but two downstage structures he included would become crucial to the production. It was never clear to me exactly what these structures were meant to represent—stone benches or ledges of some sort—and it took me a while to understand the word that the cast and crew were using for them. The "setabols?" The "citabells?" The theater people didn't really care what they represented. To them they were simply places where actors could sit down: the "sittables."

HERO ON HOT SEAT

I didn't have to wait long to understand the utility of the sittables, or the general notion that actors need spaces to act in. On the third day of rehearsal, May 8, David Frank and a few of the cast worked on act 2, scene 1, in which Beatrice expresses herself on the subject of marriage. To wit, she has no use for it. Which will put her in a difficult situation someday: when Leonato is gone, his grand estate, her home, will pass to Hero, and Beatrice will be at the mercy of Hero's husband, whoever that might be.

At first it seems that Beatrice's talk is all fun—entertainment for those within hearing, as she is wont to provide. She'd never have a man with a beard, she vows—she'd rather lie in the woollen. But a clean-shaven man, what would she do with him? "Dress him in my apparel and make him my waiting gentlewoman?" No, she will arrive a spinster at Saint Peter's gate; he will show her where in heaven the unwed souls reside, and there with them she will spend a merry eternity.

But the scene does not hold this lighthearted note. Beatrice's audience consists of Leonato, who's hoping to have the prince of Aragon for a son-in-law; Leonato's brother, Antonio, who has no patience for Beatrice's independence and no desire to be entertained; and Hero, who is mostly silent. The word is out that Don Pedro will woo Hero at a ball later tonight. Leonato has told her how to answer if the prince asks for her hand. As Beatrice banters gaily, Antonio cuts in and addresses Hero, his niece, with an abrupt change of tone. Beatrice then comes to her cousin's aid.

> **Beatrice:** . . . away to Saint Peter fore the heavens. He shows me where the bachelors sit, and there live we as merry as the day is long.
> **Antonio:** Well, niece, I trust you will be ruled by your father.
> **Beatrice:** Yes, faith, it is my cousin's duty to make curtsy and say, 'Father, as it please you.' But yet for all that, cousin, let him be a handsome fellow, or else make another curtsy and say, 'Father, as it please me.'
> **Leonato** (changing the subject from Hero's future to Beatrice's): Well, niece, I hope to see you one day fitted with a husband.

MUCH ADO

"HERO"

Beatrice: Not till God make men of some other mettle than earth. Would it not grieve a woman to be overmastered with a piece of valiant dust?—to make an account of her life to a clod of wayward marl? No, uncle, I'll none. Adam's sons are my brethren, and truly I hold it a sin to match in my kindred.

Leonato (back to Hero, changing the subject again): Daughter, remember what I told you. If the Prince do solicit you in that kind, you know your answer.

Beatrice (now addressing Hero): The fault will be in the music, cousin, if you be not wooed in good time. If the Prince be too important, tell him there is measure in everything, and so dance out the answer. For hear me, Hero, wooing, wedding, and repenting is as a Scotch jig, a measure, and a cinquepace (three types of dance). The first suit is hot and hasty, like a Scotch jig—and full as fantastical; the wedding mannerly modest, as a measure, full of state and ancientry. And then comes repentance, and with his bad legs falls into the cinquepace faster and faster till he sink into his grave.

The actors rehearsed the scene at about midstage, using their hands and moving through the space in their never-ending effort to look like real people having a conversation. But this conversation is scattered. Beatrice seems to be on one track, Antonio on another, and Leonato seems to jump back and forth between the two. Hero can only be confused. I certainly was.

But then Kelsey Brennan, who played Hero, asked for something to sit on and everything snapped into place. Frank suggested that she come downstage to where the stage-right sittable would be. At this point it was imaginary, represented by strips of tape on the rehearsal room floor, so a prop bench was produced to take its place. The next time they ran the scene it was transformed. Hero was seated with her back to the audience, looking up as the other characters talked down to her. By physically establishing herself as the focus of the scene, Brennan took the edge off the text's changes of subject. Now all the language seemed to be pointed in the same direction: to instruct Hero on the necessity (Antonio and Leonato) and the iniquity (Beatrice) of marriage. I was reminded of lawyers making their arguments at trial. Hero was the jury, but also the accused and the victim. And Beatrice's closing argument about the three stages of marriage, the dance that begins as heat and ends in chaos and cold earth, seemed to have been drained of all its wit and cleverness. As Colleen Madden came to play it, only anger was left. Her last line was no fun, all fire.

Leonato: Cousin, you apprehend passing shrewdly.
Beatrice: I have a good eye, uncle. I can see a church by daylight.

THE DANCE

―――

After Hero takes the hot seat in 2.1, the scene goes on to provide vivid proof that Shakespeare plays should be seen and not read:

> **Leonato:** Cousin, you apprehend passing shrewdly.
> **Beatrice:** I have a good eye, uncle. I can see a church by daylight.
> **Leonato:** The revellers are entering, brother. Make good room.
>
> *Enter [Don] Pedro, [the] Prince, Claudio, Benedick, and Balthasar, Don John, [and Borachio, as] Maskers, with a drum*
>
> **Don Pedro** [to Hero]: Lady, will you walk a bout with your friend?

Hero: So you walk softly, and look sweetly, and say nothing, I am yours for the walk; and especially when I walk away.

Don Pedro: With me in your company?

Hero: I may say so when I please.

Don Pedro: And when please you to say so?

Hero: When I like your favour; for God defend the lute (his face) should be like the case (his mask) . . .

Don Pedro: Speak low if you speak love.

[They move aside.]

Balthasar [to Margaret]: Well, I would you did like me.

Margaret: So would not I, for your own sake, for I have many ill qualities.

Balthasar: Which is one?

Margaret: I say my prayers aloud.

Balthasar: I love you the better—the hearers may cry amen.

Margaret: God match me with a good dancer.

Balthasar: Amen.

Margaret: And God keep him out of my sight when the dance is done. Answer, clerk.

Balthasar: No more words. The clerk is answered.

[They move aside.]

Ursula [to Antonio]: I know you well enough, you are Signor Antonio.

Antonio: At a word, I am not.

Ursula: I know you by the waggling of your head.

Antonio: To tell you true, I counterfeit him.

Ursula: You could never do him so ill-well unless you were the very man. Here's his dry hand up and down. You are he, you are he.

Antonio: At a word, I am not.

Ursula: Come, come, do you think I do not know you by your excellent wit? Can virtue hide itself? Go to, mum, you are he. Graces will appear, and there's an end.

What's happening here? The text above follows *The Norton Shakespeare*, which uses square brackets [like this] to indicate stage directions that were added by editors after the publication of the Folio of 1623 (seven years after Shakespeare's death). Imagine a first-time reader trying to understand this scene without such hints as "To Hero" or "They move aside." Even with those hints, many readers would be confused if not thoroughly discouraged.

But onstage it all makes perfect sense. It's a party. Sex is in the air. In APT's version, Leonato says, "The revellers are entering," music begins, and the soldiers come on with a lusty roar, soon joined by the ladies of the household. They dance. The men are masked, the women wary—the predators and the prey. Don Pedro, whose identity is unclear to Hero, advances on her and then draws her aside. Balthasar and Margaret now dance into view and have their exchange, establishing that Balthasar is young and eager and Margaret is something of a tease. When they move aside the focus turns to Ursula and Antonio. As Abbey Siegworth and Paul Bentzen played them, she was a fetching young lady and he a dirty old man.

In a movie this scene might consist of a wide shot intercut with successive two-shots. We'd see people dancing, or just sitting around with drinks in their hands, and then the camera would move around the room, isolating each couple's conversation as the party went on in soft focus around them. In the theater it's the audience's eyes that must move, and the job of telling them where to look must be done by the blocking or, in this case, the choreography. In APT's production this work fell to Linda Fortunato, a Chicago-based actor, director, and choreographer who was hired to make the dances for *Much Ado* and *Romeo and Juliet*.

Over winter and spring she discussed the scene with David Frank and with the composer, John Tanner. Tanner, working in his studio in Milwaukee, wrote the music, recorded a demo on piano (later he would arrange it for bass, accordion, guitar, and mandolin), and sent it to Fortunato by email. By the time she arrived in Spring Green, in the second week of rehearsal, she had fashioned a dance that followed the music, was true to the period, and moved the characters around the stage in a way that gave each couple its moment of focus as the other dancers swirled around them. To match Ursula's line about Antonio's hand—"Here's his dry hand up and down"—she included a move that fit so well I wondered if it wasn't precisely what Shakespeare had in mind. Most important, perhaps, the dance was simple enough that she could teach it to a cast of actors who had a lot of other things on their minds. She had two days.

Before the rehearsal started, the women went to a rack in the corner of the room and stepped into rehearsal skirts—voluminous, multilayered things meant to give them a sense of the space they would occupy in full costume. The choreographer showed them their moves, then Evelyn Matten punched up the music on a boom box and the dancing began as Fortunato called out the steps in 1-2-3 rhythm. "Sway, move, a-way. Sway, sway, and bow. 123 123 here-comes-the-man. 123 123 please-dance-with-me." As the cast tried to learn the steps, many faces clenched in concentration. Lines that seemed easy were coming out halting and wooden. But as the session went on and the actors became comfortable with the dance, a wonderful thing happened: they began to make up little stories for their characters to play in the background, while the audience's attention would presumably be directed elsewhere.

Balthasar, played by Robert Doyle, is stung by Margaret's flip rejection but determined to persist. The dance brings him to his next partner, who happens to be Beatrice, but he's still preoccupied with Margaret and can barely pay attention. Beatrice waves him off and dances by herself for a spell.

Ursula, the gentlewoman-in-waiting, finds herself dancing with the noble Benedick. It's a status mismatch. Abbey Siegworth played her flustered, frightened, and finally delighted as she takes the officer's arm and accepts his attention.

Beatrice sees Don Pedro leading Hero off the dance floor and watches after them apprehensively, all but ignoring her dance partner as the recent unpleasantness echoes in her mind. "Daughter, remember what I told you."

Later I asked Madden where that bit had come from: Did she make it up for herself? Had she talked about it with anyone? "No, not yet. I think most of the time I might say, David, I was thinking . . . But sometimes you make up stuff like that, and then if it doesn't work the director will say, what are you doing? And, don't do that anymore. Jim DeVita just did that to me in my other play. [He was directing *Romeo and Juliet*; Madden played Juliet's nurse.] That thing you're doing? Don't do that.

"Often you just get up there and you do the dance

and then you do your acting—but it's so much more fun if you're acting during the dance. I have to be up there, I have to be in that place, so the question I always ask is, what is my character doing? And given that we collectively have made up that Hero is the most important person to Beatrice at this point, and given the scene right before, which we are taking to suggest that all of us believe, wrongly believe, that Hero is going to be proposed to by the prince, I'm concerned, and I see a man approach her, so I'm watching. It's basically a practicality—you know, what am I doing up here?—but also it just makes it so much more interesting and fun for me. I'm probably overdoing it at the moment, but I will do less, and probably not many people will see it, but it will make sense for me."

I also asked Abbey Siegworth about the story she improvised—her fear and delight at the prospect of dancing with Signor Benedick. Her character, Ursula, does not have many lines outside the female gulling scene, and in that scene she is dissembling. An actor trying to invent a personality for her does not get much to work with. But Siegworth had thought about the role, and she seemed especially adept at acting without words—"off the line," as they sometimes say—using her face and body language to express the character she chose to present.

She decided to play Ursula as a foil to Margaret, her fellow gentlewoman-in-waiting. She reasoned that Margaret and Beatrice are something of a pair—bold and confident of what they want. She would play Ursula as one of a pair with Hero—shy, innocent, more passive.

A few days before rehearsing the dance scene, she told me, she was working on the gulling scene with Madden and Kelsey Brennan. While Beatrice hides behind the wrought-iron fence, Ursula dreamily praises Benedick so Beatrice can hear:

> Signor Benedick,
> For shape, for bearing, argument, and valour
> Goes foremost in report through Italy.

In the rehearsal room Siegworth commented that Ursula probably doesn't believe that—it's just part of the con. But Madden said wait, don't be so sure, and that gave Siegworth something to work with. "I thought yeah, what if I do have a little crush on Benedick? And so dancing with him is like a huge excitement. And also I was sort of forgetting the dance at points, so I thought oh, what if I use that? What if she forgets how to dance because she's excited? We didn't talk about it, but I just sort of let it evolve a little bit. And we practiced the dance so many times, every time was an opportunity to try something new. And if it's one of those things that David then sees and says you know, I don't think that's the right way, then I would just find

something else. We'd talk about it. But it's just trying something, letting him see it. *When* he sees it.
He's seeing other things more important right now,
but if he gets to the point where he sees the detail,
great. And if not it's just like details for us. Or for
two people in the audience that happen to catch it."

THE SHAKESPEARE INDUSTRY

I n 1939 Ivor John Carnegie Brown, a British journalist and critic, and George Fearon, his otherwise
forgotten coauthor, published *Amazing Monument:
A Short History of the Shakespeare Industry*, a book
about "a cosmic industry, which . . . seems to be
developing new phases and widening its appeal
every year." Often the term "Shakespeare industry"
is used to indicate the vast academic enterprise
inspired by Shakespeare's life and writing—all the
books and papers and footnotes and professorships
and whatnot. Sometimes the term is applied to a
subset of that enterprise devoted to the question
of whether Shakespeare was really Shakespeare or
someone else. But Brown and Fearon were aiming
at a bigger target. Their book opens on the outskirts
of Stratford-upon-Avon, at a gas station "whose

proprietor has made a gesture and an intimation. In front of his premises he displays a statue of the head of William Shakespeare. At night he reverently removes the same and gives it shelter." From this preposterous garage—"Stratford on Petrol," they call it—the authors undertake to examine an international economic engine fueled by "Bardolatry," everything from souvenir trinkets to tourist attractions to Hollywood "super-films" and beyond.

Shakespeare, they point out, was not all that when he died. "He was liked and esteemed, he became a Gentleman. He made money. He seems to have liked the money and handled it prudently." But "There was no burial in Westminster Abbey for Stratford's William, as there was for Chaucer, Spenser, Beaumont, and Jonson. A grave and a bust in the local church were his meed. . . . And there they left him, a country gentleman decently buried, with complimentary verses, among his kin and kindred. It was not until a century and a half after Shakespeare's death that the simple monument grew into a shrine, the honored name became a tradesman's talisman, the 'harlotry player' a national hero, almost a national saint, the bard an immortal, and the cult of that Immortal Bard an industry which has ramifications all over the world. . . . How that monument first was slowly built and how it is being incessantly enlarged we hope, in the following chapters, to describe and to explain."

They describe plenty but don't succeed in explaining much. Already by 1939, evidently, the Shakespeare industry was so vast that the authors could not really measure it, they could only suggest its extent by anecdotes in which outlandishness served as a proxy for magnitude. Often the outlandishness is American in origin. In their opening chapter the authors expend about a page and a half recounting the pains taken in Stratford-upon-Avon to comply with a request received by cable in 1936: "Please send earth Shakespeare's Garden and water River Avon for dedication Shakespeare Theatre, Dallas, Texas, July 1st." Texas of all places! Then they confide:

> The addiction of mankind to relics and the belief
> that some especial grace may be communicated
> by contact therewith is common in all religions,
> Bardolatry not least. We have ourselves noticed in
> Stratford's parish church, after the announcement
> by some unscrupulous guide that Shakespeare
> was here a choirboy and sat in a certain stall, the
> thrill of excitement which animated the bosoms,
> even the entire frames, of a conducted party of
> young American womanhood. Dallas may worship
> afar the transported elements of Stratford's soil
> and river: these, blessed above women, were on
> the actual spot, and there had the opportunity
> to "contact"—as they themselves would have

said—Shakespeare's reputed seat. "Contact" it they most eagerly did, each placing her rump for one glorious moment on the sacred oak and evidently deriving—such was the air of rapture on each face—a sense of inspiration, of instant and glowing community with genius, *a posteriori.*

Toward the end of their book Messrs. Brown and Fearon deploy some statistics from George Cukor's 1936 film *Romeo and Juliet,* which starred Norma Shearer and Leslie Howard. This production, they note with eyebrows cocked, required some "60,000 square feet of plaster, 75,000 feet of heavy lumber, 35,000 feet of composition board, 24,000 pounds of tiling, 20,000 yards of cloth, 90,000 flagstones, 60 trees, 100 pigeons, 500 lipsticks, 40 Veronese ducats, and hundreds of jewelled daggers. Miss Shearer, despite all this, made an effective Juliet and the civil strife of Verona was vigorously portrayed. Above all, of course, the crimson glory of those 500 lipsticks burns in the mind for ever."

Here in the 21st century we have more scientific tools of analysis—or at least we have tools that can be used to create the illusion of science. Recently I searched Google Books for titles containing "Shakespeare" and found some 52,600 items—not as many as "Jesus" (94,200), but more than Buddha, Mohammed (and Muhammad), and Yahweh put together. Also more than baseball, basketball, football, soccer, television, the Beatles, and Elvis, though not as many as sex (66,600).

Another tool we have is Google Maps. Here's one from the Institute of Outdoor Theatre showing Shakespeare festivals around the world.

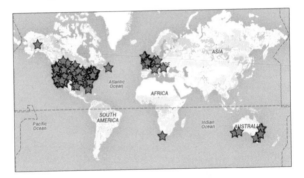

These, I hasten to point out, are outdoor theaters only. The Institute places every outdoor theater it can find into one of four categories—Shakespeare festivals, religious plays (pageants, etc.), historical plays (including reenactments), and musicals-plays (summer stock, spectacles, miscellaneous). The Shakespeare category accounts for nearly half the 385 venues listed. Meanwhile a trade group, the Shakespeare Theatre Association, counts 155 dues-paying member companies, most of which are prosperous enough to send at least one staffer to the association's main event, an annual convention. According to these sources there's a Colorado Shakespeare Festival, an Illinois Shakespeare Festival, a

Kentucky Shakespeare Festival, and a South Dakota Shakespeare Festival. There are Shakespeare festivals in Cleveland, Seattle, Houston, and Richmond, Indiana. There's Shakespeare in the Park, Shakespeare in Delaware Park, Pittsburgh Shakespeare in the Parks, and Shakespeare in Clark Park; Shakespeare in the Ruff, Shakespeare in the Ruins, Shakespeare in the Vines, Shakespeare in the Valley, and Shakespeare Napa Valley, as well as Bard in the Botanics and Bard on the Beach in Canada, not to be confused with Bard on the Beach in Australia, or Shakespeare by the Sea, or Salty Shakespeare, to name just a handful.*

American Players Theatre is near the top of this list in terms of tickets sold and annual budget. In North America the biggest Shakespeare companies are the Stratford Festival in Stratford, Ontario, and the Oregon Shakespeare Festival in Ashland; they reported attendance of 462,000 and 398,000 respectively in 2014, and budgets of about $57 million and $34 million. APT is in the next tier, which also includes Bard on the Beach in Vancouver and the Utah Shakespeare Festival in Cedar City; they each sell roughly 100,000 tickets a year and have budgets in the range of $5-$7 million.

* Map courtesy of the Institute of Outdoor Theatre, www .outdoor-theatre.org. The Shakespeare Theatre Association is at www.stahome.org.

Note that it doesn't take a metropolis to make a successful Shakespeare company. The Stratford Festival was founded in 1952 specifically to capitalize on the name of the city, which had been laid low by the decline of its furniture and railroad industries. Today Stratford is permanent home to fewer than 31,000 people. The Oregon Shakespeare Festival was founded in 1935, when the population of Ashland was less than 5,000; today it's barely more than 20,000. The Utah Shakespeare Festival, founded in 1961, is affiliated with Southern Utah University in Cedar City, population 29,000. APT's home, Spring Green, has a population of fewer than 2,000. That these companies can draw hundreds of thousands of playgoers every year, and inspire the kind of loyalty and repeat business they enjoy and the philanthropy on which they all rely to one extent or another, is due no doubt to a number of factors, including their longevity and persistence, marketing and promotional skills, the talent of their artists and artisans, and a lot of luck. But it's also due, surely, to our insatiable appetite for stories that explain us to ourselves, and to Shakespeare's unique ability to tell those stories in language built for the ages. Even Messrs. Brown and Fearon have to agree. On the last page of their book they finally surrender their snark and admit that "The existence of a Shakespeare Industry is not only inevitable: it is desirable."

Were there no Shakespeare shrines, no dramatic
festivals, no proper care of his boyhood places, his
garden and his grave, no Birthday offerings of flag
and flower as well as performance of his written
word, the world would deem us to be thankless
barbarians, unworthy of our fortune. . . . We trust
that where we have smiled at the Industry the
laughing mood was justified and that, where honour was due for honourable homage to the greatest
of all our poets, playwrights, and masters of the
English tongue, we have duly paid debt to the good
servitors of Shakespeare's name.

I'm not personally familiar with APT's peer
companies or its betters, but I have been seeing
Shakespeare in Spring Green for many years, and
I am familiar with the people sitting around me.
Many of them are from Madison, Wisconsin, a city
of academics and techies and government workers,
well-educated people who probably attend theater
more than most. But many others are dairy farmers
and contractors, high school kids and stay-home
moms, farm implement dealers and secretaries and
tourists and cops and plumbers who learned to love
theater by coming to APT on a whim or a lark or
under duress. Like me, they saw a Shakespeare play
presented well and thought to themselves, *Oh! So
that's what all the fuss is about.*

TRUE REP

——

APT is one of a dying breed in the United States: a true repertory company of actors and artisans presenting a number of plays in rotation. At season's peak they offer as many as ten performances over a three-day weekend, eight different plays in afternoon and evening shows on their main "Up the Hill" stage (1,148 capacity) and in the indoor Touchstone Theatre (201). The company sells almost half its tickets in and around Madison, roughly an hour away, and another 40 percent to farther-flung customers driving from places like Milwaukee (two hours), Chicago (three and a half), and Minneapolis (four). Although there is not much tourist infrastructure in Spring Green, many APT patrons come to see as many plays as they can cram into a two- or three-day visit. It pays to have a lot going at once. But it also means an unusual amount of work for the actors and stage managers. In the 2014 season most actors were in two shows in June and three by mid-August.

The company had seven weeks to learn the first five plays, and enough rehearsal spaces (although some were makeshift) so that scenes from all five could be going at any given moment. Scenes were rehearsed individually, for the most part, in whatever order they could be scheduled. Only toward the end of spring were they strung together into full running plays. The schedule had to be painstakingly assembled to avoid conflicts and make the most of the actors' time.

Days were organized into "rehearsal blocks," typically two per day of four hours each. In each block, one or two shows were "primary," meaning their directors had first claim on the company: they could call the whole cast or any actors they wanted. Those who were not called for the primary rehearsal were then available for secondary and, after that, tertiary rehearsals. Months ago the shows had been cast with these requirements in mind—in pairs, roughly, so that most of the actors who had big roles in *Much Ado* had smaller roles or none at all in *Romeo and Juliet*.

Saturday, May 17, was the eleventh day of rehearsal. The afternoon block from noon to 4 p.m. was given first to *Romeo and Juliet* (*R&J* in the company shorthand) and *The Year of Magical Thinking*. These two could share the primary block because the latter, a one-woman show based on the memoir by Joan Didion, starred actress Sarah Day, who had no role in *R&J*. The evening rehearsal block, 6 to 10 p.m., was given to *The Importance of Being Earnest* and *American Buffalo*. They had also been cast and scheduled deliberately to avoid conflicts—not too difficult in this case because *American Buffalo* needs only three actors.

The day before, Evelyn Matten had met with her stage-manager counterparts from the other four plays to arrange the Saturday schedule. Each stage manager had conferred with her director (all five of the stage managers were women) to determine what scenes they wanted to rehearse, and now they fit the pieces together into a tight puzzle. Jim DeVita, the director of *R&J*, wants an hour to rehearse act 2 scene 1 on the outdoor stage; the scene requires Actors A, B, C, D, and E. Meanwhile David Frank could use a chance to work some of the Beatrice-Benedick scenes in the large rehearsal room. That would require two actors, E and F. F is free all evening. So let's do *R&J* 2.1 from 7 to 8 p.m., then *Much Ado* from 8 to 10. We'll get a golf cart to shuttle E from one place to the other.

All this and more—including the union rules regarding breaks and maximum rehearsal times—was negotiated among the five stage managers and set on paper so the actors could read tomorrow's assignments on the bulletin board. The schedule was also recorded on a phone-in "rehearsal hotline": the times, the scenes or pages to be rehearsed, the actors called for each session (always referred to as Ms. or Mr.), plus all their haircuts, voice and text sessions, and wig and costume fittings, which also had to be fit into the puzzle.

This elaborate machinery delivered *Much Ado*'s lead couple, Colleen Madden and David Daniel, to the door of "LRM," the large rehearsal room, around 8 on Saturday night. Frank and Matten were there waiting for them, seated behind work tables. Frank had several editions of the play and the scale model of the set before him. Matten had a huge looseleaf binder that contained APT's working script and places for her to draw and write notes about exits, entrances, and blocking. The actors came in, pleasantries were exchanged, and at 8:10, as recorded by Matten in her book, they sat down across from the director and began to discuss their characters and the most important scene in the play.

BIG SCENE

———

Don John the bastard, having succeeded in creating only momentary havoc with his first evil plot, follows with a masterstroke. His sidekick Borachio happens to be on very friendly terms with Margaret, Hero's sexually unabashed gentlewoman-in-waiting. Knowing his master's appetite for trouble, Borachio volunteers that he and Margaret can enact an amorous encounter at the window of Hero's bedroom—an encounter that Don John brings Claudio and Don Pedro to witness on the eve of the much-anticipated wedding. In what could be called the play's third gulling, the soldiers believe they see the bride-to-be keeping company with a ruffian. In the world of this play, few fears are greater than men's fear of female sexuality; anxious jokes about horns and cuckoldry abound. So when Claudio and

Don Pedro see what they think is Hero's midnight tryst, they resolve to shame her the next morning at the ceremony. This brings us to the wedding scene, the longest and most complicated in the play, which contains several important turns of the plot—and no wedding.

In the morning, as Leonato hands his daughter to the groom, Claudio and Don Pedro attack with gusto, proclaiming to the whole congregation that Hero is no virgin; she is instead a "rotten orange," an "approved wanton," a "common stale" who "knows the heat of a luxurious bed." Even Leonato is swept up in the ensuing panic. When the baffled and beset Hero swoons and falls to the floor, her father begs her to save him from shame. By dying.

> Do not live, Hero, do not ope thine eyes,
> For did I think thou wouldst not quickly die,
> Thought I thy spirits were stronger than thy shames,
> Myself would on the rearward of reproaches
> Strike at thy life.

The friar who was to perform the ceremony, like most of those present, has watched aghast as the nuptials have unraveled. Now he comes forward as a voice of reason. Amid all the drama, he says, he has been "noting of the lady." He's seen her blushing at the accusations—Claudio has offered her blushes as proof of her guilt—but he also has seen that "in her eye there hath appeared a fire / To burn the error that these princes hold / Against her maiden truth." That is to say, she is pissed off. Call me a fool, the friar concludes, but I say she's innocent: "There is some strange misprision in the princes."

Leonato is now thoroughly confused. "I know not. If they but speak truth of her / These hands shall tear her. If they wrong her honor / The proud-est of them shall well hear of it." (Here Shakespeare sends us a big clue about the gender politics of his time: If my daughter has been sleeping around I will tear her limb from limb. And if those soldiers are lying about her, well, well—I'll give them a piece of my mind!)

To resolve the crisis, the friar suggests a de-ception of his own. Claudio and Don Pedro have left the scene. Don John, the only character at the wedding who knew it was all a lie, urged them away as soon as Hero hit the floor. For all they know, she never got up. "Your daughter here the princes left for dead," the friar tells Leonato. "Let her a while be secretly kept in, / And publish it that she is dead indeed." This, the friar explains, will change Clau-dio's slander to remorse: "When he shall hear she died upon his words . . . Then shall he mourn." And if it turns out that Hero really is the trollop they say she is, we can always get her to a nunnery:

The supposition of the lady's death
Will quench the wonder of her infamy.
And if it sort not well, you may conceal her,
As best befits her wounded reputation,
In some reclusive and religious life,
Out of all eyes, tongues, minds, and injuries.

Leonato agrees to the friar's plan and all walk off except Beatrice and Benedick. Beatrice is sobbing for her cousin, who as a result of Claudio's calumny is now officially unfit for marriage. "Sweet Hero," she says a little later, "she is wronged, she is slandered, she is undone." Benedick approaches gingerly:

Benedick: Lady Beatrice, have you wept all this while?
Beatrice: Yea, and I will weep a while longer.
Benedick: I will not desire that.
Beatrice: You have no reason, I do it freely.
Benedick: Surely I do believe your fair cousin is wronged.
Beatrice: Ah, how much might the man deserve of me that would right her!
Benedick: Is there any way to show such friendship?
Beatrice: A very even way, but no such friend.
Benedick: May a man do it?
Beatrice: It is a man's office, but not yours.

"I do it freely." Even in grief, Beatrice wields that sharp tongue. But Benedick is solicitous. Though his brothers-in-arms have created this upset, and particularly his good friend Claudio, Benedick is thinking about switching sides. He has been thoroughly gulled and now believes that he and Beatrice are in love. Beatrice believes the same. But they have never acknowledged this to each other. Benedick is trying to offer his service, as a lover might; Beatrice is holding him off, insisting it's not his problem.

Or maybe she has something else in mind.

MAGIC MOMENT

———

Some directors, I'm told, can see it all in their heads before rehearsals begin. They can tell the actors: Stand over here. Cross stage left. Say the line this way. Turn like this.

Not David Frank. For him it's mostly about language. "You can tell where a director's feelers are out," David Daniel told me. "I've seen directors walk around the room and talk to themselves as the show's going on, because they don't need to listen; they're just watching and feeling it. On the opposite end, I've seen David in a rehearsal sit at the table and close his eyes as he's listening, because what he would see doesn't matter as much to him as what he's hearing. For him it's aural. You could put this play on radio and David would change very little of it."

Frank likes "table time": sitting across from the actors, reading the lines, dissecting the text. Why does he say it like this? What's the meaning of this image? What feeling is she expressing? Why does she feel that way? Did they have a relationship before this? What happened then?

So on Saturday, May 17, when Madden and Daniel came in to rehearse their big scenes together, they sat and talked. They read through their dialogue, picked the lines apart, discussed their implications for moments that occur earlier and later in the play. After about an hour of this Madden said, "Can we get our feet on the ground?" Meaning, can we get up from the table and start moving around, blocking it and acting it out? Often this was called "putting it on its feet." Evelyn Matten checked her watch and said, "We have about 45 minutes." Daniel exclaimed, "All right!"

The floor of the rehearsal room was marked out with long lines of colored tape—outlines of the sets, so the actors could imagine where the steps and the trees and the other features would be as they moved about the space: red tape for *R&J*'s set, purple for *Earnest*, green for *Much Ado*. Near the front of the room, a couple of benches from the prop shop now stood in for the downstage sittables.

For the most part, Frank left the actors to roam the space as they saw fit. They well knew where the power spots were—the places where they would be most visible and where the play's most important moments should take place. For the scene in which Lady Beatrice weeps and Benedick tries to comfort her, they chose downstage right at aisle four.

Madden sat herself on a bench and began to sob. She was facing what would be the right side of the house, giving her profile to the center seats. Daniel circled around her, over her, as their dialogue proceeded. "It is a man's office, but not yours." He crossed behind the bench, saying nothing, and then improvised what would become the most exquisite moment in the production. He sat down facing the back of the stage. His back was to hers, his head turned away from her and from most of the audience, as he softly spoke the line that finally proclaims his love and changes everything: "I do love nothing in the world so well as you." Long pause. "Is not that strange?"

"Ah! Ah! Ah!" That was the director, seated at his table in the front of the room, stomping all over the quiet line, "Is not that strange?" He often exclaims like this when he sees or hears something that touches him. The actors are used to it and continued their dialogue, but after a few more lines Frank could not be ignored. "Right then, OK," he interrupted. "That seems to me a moment—I love— that was so surprising! What the hell is he doing?" Daniel laughed gleefully. He knew he'd made a move that landed.

Frank: I love it.

Daniel: It's a way of getting close, physically close . . .

Frank: Without presuming.

Daniel: Yes, without presuming.

Frank: Oh, but it's also incredibly powerful and surprising! How does that feel for you, Colleen?

Months later, long after the run was over, I discussed that move with Daniel. "I may have been responsible for the embryonic moment," he said, "but it took a lot of other people to make it into something later."

His first collaborator was his acting partner Madden. As Daniel explained how they worked together, I understood in a concrete way what actors mean by their constant talk of trusting one another.

"I had no idea what was going to happen, which happens with a lot of choices in rehearsal. You just have to trust yourself. And Colleen's trusting me. She's like, why is it so quiet, what's he doing?"

She can't see him and doesn't know what he's up to. Is he waiting for her to do something? Has he forgotten his line? She could easily have killed the moment and it would have disappeared forever. "She's doing her thing; she's free to do something not knowing if she's going to interrupt me or not. But she trusts me; she's going to hold her moment."

Daniel told me that when he came into the rehearsal, he had a different choice in mind. "I had one in my back pocket; I was saying oh, I can't wait to use this. When I was cast as Benedick I thought, I know exactly how I'm going to do it. It was to take her and kiss her as hard as I could, and then put her down and say, I do love nothing in the world so well as you. Is not that strange? And it just felt like that's the thing, it's going to be great, I've got it right here. I didn't talk to anybody about it; I was just waiting for the right moment in rehearsal where I could bust it out.

"I never got a chance to do it."

What made him sit down instead? "I can't remember exactly, but it was probably something along the lines of, what do I say to her? I don't know what to say. I want to take her; I want to grab her. As an actor I have a hundred choices I want to do right now that I know David won't let me do, so as an actor I'm frustrated. And as the character, Benedick, I'm frustrated; he doesn't know how to express himself. So those layers are on top of each other, and then it's like: Give up! Just give up. What's the point?—says Benedick, and a little bit of David. Just sit down.

"David loved that moment. The most important line of the play, two backs." But both Davids wondered if there was a less risky way to do it. Not only was he saying the line softly, he was essentially directing it away from the audience. "It would have been easier for me to turn to her and say it. Just seeing my lips move would make a big difference for the audience. But then we would have lost this—this thing that David wanted. It was one of the hardest things I've ever done out there."

Out there meaning on APT's main stage. It's one thing to land a line in the rehearsal room, but quite another to do it outdoors, unamplified, and reach 1,100 people with it. If it's hot, the audience might be fidgety; when they move, the vinyl-covered seats will squeak against their bare skin. If it's windy, the trees will rustle, or a gust might carry your words off into the woods. If it's drizzling, or threatening to, many people will be wearing plastic ponchos that will crinkle with their every move. If the night is still and dry, your voice will carry and you can say the line a little more subtly. But if the local whip-poor-will starts up at the wrong time, your tender confession will be overwhelmed by nature's comedy.

"I'm facing upstage, away from the audience. They can't see my lips move. I have to bounce the line off the back walls of the set and speak it strong enough to hit the audience, but with a kind of quality that makes it sound like, oh it just kind of fell off his shoulders. Which is hard, to make it fall off your shoulders with 1,100 people behind you. So every night is completely different. David said to me, if we lose them, we're going to lose them. But if we get them, we've *got* them. That's on you. That's your job, to make sure those words get out there. Don't lose them. Don't lose a single person."

Matten watched the moment closely, night after night, and fed Daniel notes throughout the run. "One of the things that Ev told me was to make sure that *Colleen* could hear it. Which of course just makes perfect sense, why didn't I think of this? In my actor's brain I was always concerned about the audience hearing it and working on that, but when I'm worried about the audience I lose the intimacy between the two of us, and it just becomes very wide and loud and bland. Ev knew my actor instincts would make sure the audience could hear it. When she told me to make sure *Beatrice* can hear it, you're saying it to *her*, it became pointed and sharper; it had a direction and focus. That helped me take a big step in the mechanics of that moment."

So what percentage of the time did you nail it? I asked. He defined "nail it" as giving everyone in the audience the same experience. Then he was silent for a long time. Finally he said about two-thirds: "About a third of the time, roughly, I felt like I missed the mark."

KILL CLAUDIO

———

The scene continues:

Benedick: I do love nothing in the world so well as you. Is not that strange?

Beatrice: As strange as the thing I know not. It were as possible for me to say I loved nothing so well as you, but believe me not, and yet I lie not. I confess nothing nor I deny nothing. I am sorry for my cousin.

Benedick: By my sword, Beatrice, thou lovest me.

Beatrice: Do not swear and eat it.

Benedick: I will swear by it that you love me, and I will make him eat it that says I love not you.

Beatrice: Will you not eat your word?

Benedick: With no sauce that can be devised to it. I protest I love thee.

Beatrice: Why, then, God forgive me.

Benedick: What offence, sweet Beatrice?

Beatrice: You have stayed me in a happy hour. I was about to protest I loved you.

Benedick: And do it with all thy heart.

Beatrice: I love you with so much of my heart that none is left to protest.

Benedick: Come, bid me do any thing for thee.

Beatrice: Kill Claudio.

We can't know for sure, because we have almost nothing in Shakespeare's own hand, but he seems to have written very little in the way of stage directions. He had no use for them: he was writing for performance, not posterity, and as the plays were developed he was there to tell the actors whatever he wanted them to know. The Folio texts, which were assembled by Shakespeare's colleagues after his death, are marred by errors and inconsistencies and give only the most rudimentary directions—exits and entrances, mostly, and not nearly all the exits and entrances that the lines imply. In many cases (as we saw back in the act 2 dance), scholars and editors have had to interpolate the comings and goings, as well as such directions as "aside" or "To Hero." Even then it's sometimes impossible to know which character or characters are supposed to be hearing a line. Or, to put it another way, it's up to directors and actors to decide which character a line is addressed to—and how and when and whether to walk upstage, stand or sit down, pick up a prop, fall silent, shout, kiss, or crash to the floor. This is one reason for Shakespeare's enduring appeal: so much is amenable to interpretation and renewal.

"Kill Claudio" is a case in point. All Shakespeare gives us is these two words—one of the most important lines in the play. Four hundred years later, the question is not so much *how should it be played?* as *how do you want to play it?*

David Frank and the actors wanted to play it serious. And yet they knew the audience would probably find it hilarious. Colleen Madden, who had done the play twice before in smaller roles, said she never understood it as a laugh line. But David Daniel, who had done it at least three times, said the audience never fails to laugh. Frank admitted he laughed himself whenever he heard it, though mostly from surprise, and he never found the reaction very satisfying. At one point he asked hopefully, "We will—yes?—kill the most famous laugh line in the play?" It was wishful thinking, but a goal worth working toward. *Much Ado* always was and always would be full of laughs, Frank knew, but he saw more to it than that, and he wanted to play it all.

Modern audiences don't readily grasp the implications of the line the way Shakespeare's contemporaries would have. Claudio, Benedick's best buddy, has slandered Beatrice's blood relative. Hero must be avenged. It's Sicily, after all. To exact the vengeance is not a woman's office, and this enrages Beatrice: "O God that I were a man!" she cries. "I would eat his heart in the market place." But where's the man to do it for her? Her uncle Leonato is no help; a few minutes ago he was threatening to thrash his own daughter. If only Beatrice had a brother to fight for her. Or a husband. Or a fiancé.

Or a man who professes to love her.

She grills Benedick to assess the depth of his commitment. "Will you not eat your word?" And when he swears he won't, she says "Why, then, God forgive me." Why does she say that? And what does she mean by, "You have stayed me in a happy hour?" These questions were discussed in the rehearsal room, but I never had the sense that they were answered conclusively. My reading is that Beatrice is deliberately luring Benedick into a commitment whose implications are not yet clear to him. It's not that professing his love has made the hour happy for her; it's that the profession has come at just the right hour: just when she needs it. She needs someone to kill Claudio. Really.

Benedick, who has just invited her to "bid me do anything for thee," didn't really mean it. He recoils immediately, and the couple have their first argument. Like many arguing couples, they talk about two different things: Beatrice rails against the injustice done to her cousin, while Benedick keeps insisting that he loves her—what could be more important than that? Finally, even as she tries to pull herself away from this disappointing oaf, Beatrice makes her point:

> **Benedick:** Tarry, good Beatrice. By this hand, I love thee.
> **Beatrice:** Use it for my love some other way than swearing by it.
> **Benedick:** Think you in your soul the Count Claudio hath wronged Hero?
> **Beatrice:** Yea, as sure as I have a thought or a soul.
> **Benedick:** Enough, I am engaged, I will challenge him. I will kiss your hand, and so I leave you. By this hand, Claudio shall render me a dear account. As you hear of me, so think of me.

In other words, remember me fondly, I might not be back. In 21st-century America we can easily underestimate the gravity of this challenge, but Beatrice and Benedick both know the drill: Benedick must either kill his best friend or be killed himself. He is as engaged as he can be (and in two senses of the word).

Madden and I talked about "Kill Claudio" in her kitchen one Friday morning during the run. She was multitasking: while her husband, James Ridge, talked with a designer in the front room—he was set to direct a play in Madison in a few months—she was making a cake for a sick friend, submitting to an interview, and fielding multiple mom calls from one of her two sons. "We never meant it to be a laugh line," she said. Of course she had seen productions and films of the play in addition to doing it herself, but the audience reaction to the line had never made much of an impression on her. "I guess I never saw it. Never tuned into it. And David Daniel and I have been asking, do we resist that? I'm going to try something tomorrow, I think. Or I may wait till a non-Saturday to do it. Where I say 'Kill Claudio' a little earlier. Just to see if—but I don't know, maybe it's supposed to be a laugh line."

Maybe Shakespeare did want a big laugh. Maybe he was happy to have it both ways. He's allowed, he's Shakespeare. In any case, over the course of the season I saw Madden try a few different things. In rehearsals she held the line off, preceding it with three deep breaths, as though steeling herself for what she was about to ask. By the time the first preview was over she knew that wasn't working, so then she tried speeding it up. But whatever she did the line produced a big laugh. It was surefire.

THE TROUSERS DILEMMA

O n Sunday, May 18, the day after David Daniel first sat down to profess Benedick's love, he and Colleen Madden and David Frank worked the scene again. They discussed Benedick's shifting loyalty. As the scene starts he stands with Claudio and Don Pedro, his brothers-in-arms. By the time it ends, he is in Beatrice and Hero's camp. It's a Sicilian blood feud, Frank said. In professing his love for Beatrice, Benedick is switching families.

They ran through the scene, stopped and talked, ran through again and talked some more. Frank was very pleased. "We're going to end up keeping a lot of that, I hope. . . . I think we're making real progress. . . . Good-work good-work good-work." By this time Daniel was falling to his knees at the line, "Come, bid me do anything for thee." Madden was looking down to him when she said, "Kill Claudio." Frank liked the kneel.

But Evelyn Matten saw a problem. About an hour into the session, she piped up from her spot in the corner of the room. Although she is present for virtually every minute of rehearsals, she does not speak often. When she does, everyone listens.

> **Matten:** I would be remiss if I didn't say we have to be careful of how much moving on the knees we're doing.
> **Daniel:** Thank you. Am I moving on my knees?
> **Matten:** Yes. When she's turning you're spinning on your knees.

There followed a couple minutes of discussion about how the knee-moving could be avoided or minimized. Madden could go this way. Daniel could turn here. "But then I'm open." "I guess you're right. So you hit the diagonal, I'll go here . . ."

They were grappling with what Frank later called the "trousers dilemma." It's a special problem for outdoor theaters, he said, particularly in the Midwest, where it rains often in summer. Some of APT's shows have to be played on a wet stage—during a light drizzle or after a rain delay. Lest the actors slip and injure themselves, grit is mixed into the black paint that covers the stage, giving the surface the texture of coarse sandpaper. For this reason the costume shop takes extra pains to protect the hems of long skirts, capes, and dresses. Another concern is gentlemen's pants, if the gentleman in question spends much time on the floor. By the second week of rehearsal it was apparent that David Daniel would be spending a lot of time on the floor—in his love scene with Beatrice and especially during his gulling scene, in full-lazzi mode. So Matten was addressing the trousers dilemma. The knee movement: "It will destroy your pants," she said.

In fact Daniel's pants had been an issue almost from the moment planning began in the spring. At one point there was talk of making some heavy-duty pants that he could change into before the gulling scene. In the end the costume people decided it would be easier simply to order several spare pairs of his regular trousers. They started with three, and that turned out to be pants enough.

BLUE COLLAR

Brian Mani, a veteran of APT's core company, played Leonato in *Much Ado* and Donny in David Mamet's *American Buffalo*. He has a deep, resonant voice and a rare ability to elucidate Shakespearean grammar as he speaks, making arcane language clear and understandable even to novice ears. The clipped, staccato language of Mamet was new to him. At rehearsals he usually wore cargo pants with pockets on each thigh, carrying one script on one side and one on the other. During breaks in the *Much Ado* sessions, he'd prowl the parking lot outside, quietly running his lines from *American Buffalo*. Sometimes when the actors were scattering at the end of a rehearsal, he'd announce in his practiced Chicagoese that he was now on his way to a *Buffalo* session: "Arright, ahm goanda

MUCH ADO

"LEONATO"

Shick-AH-go, ahl be back tannite." Routinely, and sometimes within a matter of minutes, he went from this:

> But mine, and mine I loved, and mine I praised,
> And mine that I was proud on, mine so much
> That I myself was to myself not mine,
> Valuing of her—why she, O she is fallen
> Into a pit of ink, that the wide sea
> Hath drops too few to wash her clean again,
> And salt too little which may season give
> To her foul-tainted flesh.

to this:

Donny: Now lookit Fletcher.

Bobby: Fletch?

Donny: Now Fletcher is a standup guy.

Bobby: Yeah.

Donny: I don't *give* a shit. He is a fellow stands for something—

Bobby: Yeah.

Donny: You take him and you put him down in some strange town with just a nickel in his pocket, and by nightfall he'll have that town by the balls. This is not talk, Bob, this is action.

Bobby: He's a real good card player.

Donny: You're fucking A he is, Bob. And this is what I'm getting at.

It was as though Mani had to rehearse in two different languages. I asked him if that was especially difficult, and he answered that the extreme difference actually made it easier for him to move from one world to the other. If he were doing Leonato and Lord Capulet—two fathers who threaten their daughters in iambic pentameter—*that* would be difficult.

Which is not to say he finds it easy playing two or three roles at the same time. Donny, the main character of three in *American Buffalo*, never leaves the stage. In *Much Ado*, Leonato is in nine of seventeen scenes and has several major speeches. "Trying to absorb Donny in *Buffalo*, and trying to absorb the Leonato that David wants in *Much Ado*, it's hard work," Mani said. "A lot of people have the idea of Hollywood, and stars. They hear you're an actor, they immediately go *Oooo*, those people. We're not those people! We work long hours, and we work with tough text, and we have to struggle with the meanings, and we have to perform it in front of an audience. It's blue-collar work. You leave that show exhausted. *American Buffalo* exhausts me, maybe more mentally than physically. There's a tension that goes through it, and after the show, my legs are tired and it feels so good to have my brain free, free of having to hang on to what's being said and respond.

"The test will be—and I don't know where it is, I haven't looked on the calendar—the interesting thing will be to do a Mamet in the afternoon on a Saturday and then to do *Much Ado* that night at 8. Those two-show days can be physically demanding. But on the flip side they can be really fun to do—because you get to play two different things. Sometimes you get to play the villain and the lover, or the good uncle and the shyster who's trying to steal people's purses. And that's fun."

Mani grew up in the very small town of Winslow, Illinois, just over the Wisconsin border. It's safe to say that no one there expected him to become a Shakespearean actor. He was big and athletic; in high school he played "all the sports"—football, basketball, track, baseball in the summer. When he graduated he had no real goals or ambitions. "I started working on a farm. And my parents were both factory workers, so I figured I would work on a farm for a while, then I might work in a factory. I had no idea."

His father was one of ten children, his mother one of twenty. Neither of them was much interested in the arts, Mani told me, but they did enjoy singing and passed on to him a love of music. Whenever he had the chance he would take a choir class in school, and he performed in a couple of student musicals. "I think not many guys wanted to do it, and I got talked into it, but I guess I have enough of an extroverted character that I was fine with it.

"The fall after I graduated high school, I heard

about a production of *Man of La Mancha* that was going on down in Freeport, at the junior college [Highland Community College in Freeport, Illinois]. *La Mancha* was a play that we studied as literature in English class, and I'd seen the show. I got cast as the smallest role in the show, one of the muleteers, and I was still working on the farm. And every night when 'The Impossible Dream' started and everyone kind of one by one started raising up in the prison, I would start crying. Something about that accumulation of the emotion, and the music and the audience and the sharing of the story—whatever, all of it—just hit me like a ton of bricks. To the point that I would avoid people after the show, because I was welled up and I didn't want them to see that I was moved like that. But that's what made me decide to pursue acting.

"So I took a dance class, I took a basic acting class that next semester, and I started doing more plays, and I found that I could be successful at it. And then thank God the head of the theater department did a Shakespeare every year, so I got introduced to Shakespeare, something that I couldn't even read in high school, 'cause I didn't care. Suddenly my first role was Buckingham in *Richard III*—it's a huge role!—and it came to me easily. I understood it and it made sense to me—performing it rather than just reading and studying it."

In the mid-1980s Sandy Robbins's Professional

Theatre Training Program was still based at the University of Wisconsin at Milwaukee. Mani auditioned and was accepted as one of 36 members of a three-year class. (James DeVita was one of his classmates.) He landed at APT in 1991—Randall Duk Kim's last year. "He was a presence that was— it's like an animal walked onstage and you are just looking at it not knowing what it's going to do. And then he would do it. He just really had whatever that is. One of my instructors whom I'd worked with in Milwaukee came and saw *Tartuffe*; I was playing Cléante in that production. He said Brian, you're working with one of the top ten, maybe top five actors on this planet. Get as much as you can from this man. But there was a day when Randy gave this speech in which he said I'm tired, I'm tired, and I want everyone to know that if you're looking for inspiration from me I don't know that I can provide it. He wasn't very tutorial in those days, as I think he was in the past, but I learned a lot from him just by watching."

When that season ended, David Frank took over and Mani's APT career was derailed. "He conducted exit interviews. I could tell I was not going to be back." Mani auditioned several times over the next few years, "and then I felt I was knocking on a door that wasn't going to open, so I stopped auditioning."

But he did a "strategic thing" in 1997. "I took a job in Platteville, at the Wisconsin Shakespeare

Festival. I was the only Equity actor there; the rest were grad students from around the country. I did Leontes in *The Winter's Tale*, and then we did *Troilus and Cressida* and I played Pandarus in that production. And Brenda DeVita came to see both, and David came to see *Troilus and Cressida*, out of curiosity I think about the play, to see how stage-worthy it was, and I think partly to see me. And he has told me since that it was the first time he saw me able to win an audience over, to get them to watch my character. And I think that was what put the nugget in his head that they ought to have me there sometime. It ended up being two more years, and then lo and behold in the winter of 1999–2000 I got a call from Roseann Sheridan, who was the associate artistic director then, sort of David's right-hand person, and she said David wants to read you for a play. So I came in, read, got in, and I never left."

Just a few days before the opening of *Much Ado*, Mani felt he was still reaching for the complete Leonato. "I don't think I'm 100 percent on to what David wants. But the season is not a race, it's a marathon. There is a race to open it, but then we will do this a lot, and the audience will inform us what is working and what isn't. So as much as I've worked on Leonato, I would say in the next three or four weeks he'll change some more. I'll still be going for the same stuff, but the way I go about it will be a little different."

By that time I had heard many actors say that the audience tells them what is working. I asked Mani how this communication happens. He's concentrating on his movement, his lines, his fellow actors. How does he know what the audience is thinking? He said, "There are times when something awful happens. I think when Don John, right before the intermission when he's warning Claudio and Don Pedro about Hero, he says something awful about her and I heard an audible *Oooo* from the audience. You know that they're listening then. But there are times you can hear the silence. There are times when something has happened and you can hear a pin drop; you just hear this lack of sound, and you know that all the ears are perked. Time has stopped for a second, and you just know they're going to hang on the next ten syllables you say. You can feel that. When the focus of a scene is going well, when something is happening down here but somebody does a thing upstage, or another person comes in on a scene and you feel the heads go over to that and then come back to you, you know they're there. And that's a pretty lovely feeling."

THE DIRECTOR

———

David Frank was born in Ireland and educated in English schools, where his interest in literature and history blossomed into a passion for Shakespeare. He attended Rose Bruford College, a theater school in London, and upon graduating was offered a job he found easy to turn down: five pounds a week, small acting parts, and a lot of prop-wrangling in a small theater hours north of the city. "My alternative was a free trip to the US," Frank said. His father was a military attaché at the British embassy in Washington, DC. David hadn't seen his folks for a few years, so he decided to spend the summer with them before resuming his job hunt in England.

He already knew he was not going to be a successful actor. "There was always a little voice in me, talking to myself from the outside, saying *I think you look rather stupid.* Or, *are you sure? That seems like pretty rotten acting.* Well if you want a self-fulfilling prophecy, that's it. If you're an actor thinking I'm feeling rather stupid up here, you can be guaranteed you will look it."

Nonetheless he wanted a life in the theater, and he found it by accident on his summer sojourn.

"I was in DC for some weeks, and it was really fun. There was a whole diplomatic culture there— offspring of diplomats—and I met all sorts of fascinating people. The State Department would allow you to work for a nonprofit organization, so I got what I thought would be a temporary job as house manager—which is senior usher—at the closest theater that would have me, Center Stage in Baltimore. The thought of a house manager with an English accent was tempting to them. The pay for them looked a very small amount; to me it looked like riches that I couldn't imagine. The next thing I knew I had an offer of a job for the next year."

He brought a few assets to the job besides his accent and willingness to work cheap. One was a kind of technical training in classical theater—vocal technique, verse-speaking, and the like—that was not then common on this side of the Atlantic. Another was an affection and knack for teaching. Plus he was young, ambitious, and up for almost anything.

"This was the mid-60s. The regional theater movement in this country was just beginning to really get going. We were young, anything was possible, and we didn't look where we were leaping; we just leapt. Center Stage had a high school touring company and a children's theater, and I was always saying, please, can I try directing something? And there were never enough people. So usually they would say, you've got an English accent and you can name most of the Shakespearean works? You've got it. So I just kind of got involved in that theater."

He met his wife, Barbara, there; they married in 1968 and they worked on children's productions together: "If the script didn't exist, we'd write it." Meanwhile he was writing grants and taking on administrative tasks. "I began to discover that I actually was a decent manager. In fact that was the aching need." There were plenty of artists around; what these fledgling theaters really wanted was someone who could run a business. Eventually Frank became the general manager. "Definition: if it wasn't specifically allocated to someone else, it was my problem. I had to learn accounting. Oh I'm terrified, but I'm excited. Can I learn accounting overnight from a library book? And the answer is if you get the right book, you can.

"Well, not quite overnight."

After five years at Center Stage, he got a call from another regional company that had started up in the 60s, the Loretto-Hilton Repertory Theatre in Saint Louis, now commonly called Saint Louis Rep.

They had fired their managing director after a disastrous budget-wrecking season and they asked Frank to apply for the job. He was just 27 when he arrived. By the end of his first year he had turned a $135,000 deficit into a $36,000 surplus; by the end of his fifth the subscription base had expanded nearly fivefold.

But as he developed a reputation as an astute executive, he was drifting away from his first love. "Mostly I was managing, fundraising, dealing with the board. Directing a little bit, but there was no time to direct. If I pulled out a text and was reading it and someone knocked on the door, my first instinct was to bury it, feeling guilty." So after eight years in Saint Louis he went to Studio Arena Theatre in Buffalo, New York—a smaller theater where he could be artistic director.

He was there for eleven years, during which time, he says, the company again went from debt to relative prosperity. But Buffalo was too close to Stratford to do much Shakespeare, and close enough to New York that Frank felt pressure to employ Broadway and TV actors past their prime—not stars, but names. It wasn't his thing. When the artistic director job opened at the Oregon Shakespeare Festival, Frank jumped to apply. Oregon Shakes (as the insiders call it) had the history, the audience, and the resources to do it right—with dramaturges, voice and text coaches, and a standing company of classically trained actors. "That's the job I'm *craving*,"

Frank recalled. "And I'm pretty sure I'm going to get it." The festival flew him out to Oregon. They got along famously. They started checking his references.

And then they hired the other guy.

"It was the biggest disappointment of my life."

Meanwhile in Wisconsin, American Players Theatre was in turmoil. In 1986 the company had announced it was disbanding due to financial difficulties. Almost immediately it was resuscitated by an outpouring of community support and a big loan from the county government. The following year one of the founders, Chuck Bright, left the company, and Randall Duk Kim gave up the title of artistic director, passing it on to another founder, Anne Occhiogrosso.

Then in 1991, as Frank interviewed in Oregon, Kim and Occhiogrosso announced unexpectedly that they were leaving APT. James "Dusty" Priebe, the fourth founder, who had left very early on but had recently returned as general manager, was phoning and faxing theater contacts all over the country, hurriedly searching for a new artistic director to plan the upcoming season. One of the people he contacted was the retiring artistic director at Oregon Shakes, who told him about the guy they hadn't hired.

So on a hot afternoon in July, just weeks after losing the job of his dreams, Frank huffed his way up APT's hill and inhaled the bouquet of their infamous porta-potties. He has told the story often: "The reek was almost visible, it was so strong." He settled into the moldy velour of one of APT's recycled movie-theater seats and watched the kind of Shakespeare the company's founders insisted on: "an extraordinary production of *The Winter's Tale*— but the longest one I had ever seen. They didn't cut a word. Not a word! In the heat of that afternoon, it couldn't have been more challenging.

"And there were 400 people listening to the entire thing—spellbound! Oh God, if I could do that . . ."

Sheldon Wilner, the managing director of APT at the time, was happy to welcome Frank aboard. "He understood money!" Wilner told me, still sounding slightly amazed 23 years later. "It's an important thing for an artistic director, and a lot of them don't." Wilner, whose forte was marketing, was growing the audience and increasing revenues but butting heads with Kim and Occhiogrosso over finances, marketing issues, and play selection. Frank and his record of commercial success looked pretty good by comparison. He knew how to cut costs and had a cheerful attitude about selling tickets. A reporter for the *Capital Times* of Madison quoted him saying he had no problem doing Shakespeare's better known and more audience-friendly plays: "If you have to prostitute yourself—what a way to go!"

years would I say hey, I think you're stopping up the process. But David has kind of invited us in as peers. I'm really not his peer. He knows miles more than I do."

Evidently Frank has learned to check himself over the years. Early in rehearsals for *Much Ado*, I found myself wondering if he had any specific ideas about staging the play or if he was just waiting for the actors to come up with some. Later it became clear that he did have ideas—a lot of them. As the rehearsals proceeded the ideas became more and more detailed and he became more aggressive about interjecting them. But in the first couple of weeks he let out a lot of rope.

In 1.3, Don John enters with Conrad, who is called his "companion" in the Folio text. Conrad is advising Don John not to be such a sourpuss. In response, Don John frankly presents his character:

> I cannot hide what I am. I must be sad when I have cause, and smile at no man's jests; eat when I have stomach, and wait for no man's leisure; sleep when I am drowsy, and tend on no man's business; laugh when I am merry, and claw no man in his humor.
>
> . . . it better fits my blood to be disdained of all than to fashion a carriage to rob love from any. In this, though I cannot be said to be a flattering honest man, it must not be denied but I am a plain-dealing villain.

Reading this dialogue off the page, and trying to imagine what might be done with it, all I can see is a pair of actors facing each other and gesticulating awkwardly in a desperate attempt to look natural. No doubt the scene has been played that way in many an amateur production. But Eric Parks and Christopher Sheard, the actors who played Don John and Conrad, worked up a bit of action that made the conversation more lifelike and the relationship more complex. Conrad comes on holding a razor; Don John has a towel over his shoulder. As they argue, Don John casts the towel off and Conrad has to pick it up. Don John sits and Conrad shaves his neck. In this rendition Conrad is a lackey; he is *presuming* to advise Don John. This the actors devised on their own with no prompting from the director (and very little from the playwright).

Parks had something more in mind for the scene: he wanted a way to set Don John apart from the other soldiers, and he thought it might do to enter smoking a cigarette. Frank had his doubts. He knew the prop was historically accurate—they were smoking cigarettes in 19th-century Europe—and he understood the actor's desire for a device. But this device was jarring. Parks's smoking mannerisms, which were completely contemporary, didn't seem to fit in the world of the play. Frank let it go while he waited for a better idea to emerge. At a production meeting in the fifth week of rehearsal, he was considering a cigar. Maybe it wouldn't even need to be lit. Bob Morgan chimed in: How about snuff? Frank thought that was a brilliant idea and proposed it to Parks, who agreed it would serve his purpose. The next time the scene was rehearsed, the cigarette was gone and Don John was snorting snuff.

To judge from the conversations I had with actors, one of the biggest obstacles they face in rehearsal is the fear of looking like a fool—trying a move or a face or a voice that not only seems stupid in terms of the character or the play, but also makes the actor look stupid as a person. This is why they talk so much about trust and confidence and taking risks. You need confidence to try something unexpected or unusual, and you need to trust that your colleagues won't laugh or put their heads in their hands if it doesn't work. So directors are always walking a fine line: as they seek to realize their vision or interpretation of a play, and to exercise their judgment about what will work on an audience, they must be careful to protect the actors' confidence.

Frank often walks this line by invoking the conceit that actors are the source of all wisdom; any ideas he may contribute are not to be taken too seriously; anything he says can be disregarded if the actors don't find it helpful.

"What you'll be looking for, I'm sure, is a place where you can slow it down. I wouldn't presume to say, but you will find it."

PROFESSIONAL TRAINING

━━━━━

I t's partly coincidence that *Much Ado*'s stage manager and three of its principal actors were former students of Sandy Robbins—but only partly. When Randall Duk Kim and company arrived in Wisconsin in 1979, Robbins had just opened the Professional Theatre Training Program at the University of Wisconsin–Milwaukee. As he tells it, the Milwaukee campus was intent on establishing an arts school that would distinguish it from the mother ship in Madison. Robbins, a young comer at the time, had been recruited to lead the theater department and encouraged to think big. He established a practical training program with an exclusive focus on classical theater. At the time there were plenty of places to learn some Shakespeare, he told me, but none with such a narrow mission: not

TV, not movies, not Broadway, just classics. "What distinguished us wasn't only that we were preparing people to do that sort of thing, but that we were seeking people whose personal goals were to earn their living in those kind of plays. That is a tiny, tiny niche." But it was a perfect fit with the fledgling company in Spring Green. "That was complete serendipity, a very happy coincidence for us. I think Randy would say the same."

By the time David Frank arrived in 1991, Robbins had received an offer he couldn't refuse and had moved the entire program to the University of Delaware. But Frank visited and held auditions there regularly. "David hired scads and scads of our graduates," Robbins said. "At one time I'm pretty sure that the majority of APT actors, or just under a majority, were graduates of our school. They were close at hand and they were available and they had the chops to do that kind of material. And in those very early days when he was fighting to keep the theater alive, David took advantage of that and offered them great opportunities they might not have had elsewhere."

I asked Robbins what chops it takes to do that kind of material. What are the special demands of Shakespearean theater? What does a classical actor need to know that other actors don't? "I have to say this is all opinion, but my view is that language is the principal difference. You know, the only Shakespeare we've got is those words. Words and how they are spoken and how they land for the listener, that's 90 percent of the meaning in those plays. There are many, many more words being spoken in a Shakespearean production, for instance, than there are in a contemporary play. And at a much faster rate. And so the weapon of a professional stage actor in those plays is what they say and how they say it, more than their facial expressions or pauses or any other thing. Nothing is more important than how they speak: the variety that they're capable of vocally, the degree to which they are masterful at rhythm—because the plays that are written in verse are written in a predetermined rhythm. David Mamet may be very rhythmic—in fact he is—but he doesn't dictate the number of syllables per line, things like that. The formal requirements are way way greater. If you don't meet those formal requirements, you'll be less comprehensible and less affecting. And to meet them you need either instruction or practice at least. I don't know that you need training, because for the majority of the history of the theater there were no schools, and people learned by watching and imitating, and that seemed to work every bit as well, maybe better, than schools. But there has to be some model to emulate—you can't just get up and do it.

"Some passages in Shakespeare, for instance, are incomprehensible if they are not spoken on a single breath. They're written to keep going, they seats to sell, and that presents another challenge to the actors.

"You need to be louder, without effort. So you can sound intimate to a thousand or more people. They all think you're whispering to your lover, but some of them are 50 feet away. That's a technique, to speak the way that Benedick and Beatrice do in that church scene, the one that ends, Kill Claudio. That's a fairly intimate scene. They're in a church. And they have to be audible to 1,100 people. That's abnormal; that's weird. Almost nobody is born knowing how to do that. It takes instruction and/or practice. But a contemporary play, where the utterances are short and easy, and you're playing in smaller spaces for the most part, you don't need to be so good at that."

Robbins's Professional Theatre Training Program is defunct, eliminated by a budget-minded university president in 2011. It was an expensive undertaking; what lured him from Milwaukee in the first place was Delaware's willingness to provide tuition for all the program's students. Now Robbins is the producing artistic director of the university's Resident Ensemble Players, a professional company made up mostly of graduates and faculty from the program.

Much has changed since he started, he told me. "The American profession was very different, in a few really significant ways, one of which was there were a great many theaters with resident companies of actors year round that predominately did classic

plays or at least did a large number of them annu-
ally. And they needed people trained this way. The
profession had a hunger for such people. When I
graduated from Carnegie, which was where I studied, every single member of my graduating class of
actors was offered a year-round season's contract
at some theater—every one of us! If I say that to
people today they look at me like I'm from Mars."

WOMAN IN A RED DRESS

———

For Bob Morgan, who designed the costumes as well as the set, the first scene was all-important. In the theater, he told me, first impressions are even more powerful than in real life. Make a mistake here and the character might never recover. Hero is a girl: innocent, expectant, and a vision of such beauty that Claudio falls for her immediately. Beatrice, on the other hand, must be a woman: formidable, smart, experienced, skeptical about the simplicity of young love. All of this needs to be said in an instant, without words.

Morgan put Hero in a dress of Swiss organdy that was "all fluffy, like a peach parfait." For Beatrice, he saw red.

"Color is the most powerful tool we have as designers," Morgan said. "You put a woman in a red dress, a green dress, or a blue dress, you have three different responses. No matter what the silhouette, no matter what the detail, no matter what the period."

He thought for a while about dressing Beatrice in green for the first scene, but to him that translates as distant and standoffish. "Audience members would not go to Beatrice and embrace her the way I thought they should." He also thought about putting her in brown. "She's not expecting the men to be there, she's just going to pick herbs in the countryside or something, so she's just in a plain brown dress. But then the demands of the play are that in the first scene she has to be very vivacious and very clever and very entertaining and men find her extremely attractive. There's a high degree of witty repartee and interaction. We know that she is a creature of great emotional and intellectual energy. So I can't go with a brown dress, it's just too dreary. It didn't give her enough help, didn't support her emotionally."

In his research Morgan ran across a photo of Claudia Cardinale in the Luchino Visconti film *Il Gattopardo* (English title *The Leopard*), which was set in Sicily in the 1860s. There he saw the color he wanted. "I said let's give her something with more energy. Not a vivid red, she's not a gypsy, but a dark Indian red. It's a deep shade, and it has warmth to it. I think it communicates maturity. But the color is vibrant like her soul, and her character."

For the silhouette he wanted something very

simple. "I think it's really important that Beatrice does not dress for anybody but herself. She doesn't dress for the men; she doesn't dress for the other women. She's independent. She's made her life without a man so far. She needs to be strong and secure in her own personality. The dress needs to say I don't care about fancy. I'm beautiful in my own right because of who I am and how I think. And if I'm physically attractive—and I am—that's fine but I'm not trying to enhance it." He expressed his ideas in a line drawing and sent it off to Wisconsin with 24 others.

"Now the fabric that I bought actually isn't quite the color I wanted, but I couldn't find it in the right weight, and so I settled for this color, which has a little more blue in it; it's a little more burgundy. I think it will be OK. I definitely wanted that texture and weight. It's a linen gauze, which has a sort of everyday commonality to it—it's not satin, it's not dress-up—and it's a very hard fabric to find. I searched for three days in New York for that fabric, and this was the only piece I found that was even close to being right. Even if the color wasn't perfect. I could have put it in a dye vat and tried to strip it and overdye it, but it's got some glue in it, sizing, that keeps it a little crisper and from being too nubby, and I knew that if we processed it in a dye vat I would lose all of that quality. So I just decided to stay with the color."

Morgan has learned not to fret about finding the perfect color. "Stage lighting changes things so much. If you get frantic about it you're fooling yourself, because you don't really know what you're going to end up seeing."

—

Early in May, as rehearsals got underway, April McKinnis began the process of turning the fabric into a costume. McKinnis is a "draper," one of the costume shop elite. Her job was to supervise the making of the dress (and all the costumes in the show) and to begin the process by translating Bob Morgan's drawing into sewing patterns. In the end the dress and the drawing would not look very similar except in overall profile, but McKinnis and Morgan have been working together a long time. She knows what is essential in the drawing and what is fanciful; she can look at it and read Morgan's mind.

The first step is draping, a process that turns the two-dimensional drawing into a three-dimensional garment. McKinnis chose an inexpensive fabric that would hang on the body approximately as the red linen would—in this case, as in many others, a cotton canvas—and draped it over a dress form that was an exact replica of Colleen Madden. Using Morgan's drawing as her guide, she cut pieces of the fabric and pinned them to the dummy and to each

other to form the bodice of the dress. When she had
it fitting right she used a black Sharpie to mark the
places where one piece of canvas joined another—
the seam lines—then reduced the three dimensions
back to two: removing the canvas from the form,
she cut it into pieces along her pen lines, spread the
pieces onto a sheet of craft paper, and traced their
shapes to the paper, refining her rough lines with
the help of steel rulers called French curves.

Now the paper could be cut into patterns and
passed to the next artisan in line, the "first hand,"
who used the patterns to cut new pieces of canvas
and then sewed the pieces together to produce a
mockup of the dress, using very large stitches that
could easily be removed. This iteration was what
Madden tried on at her first fitting. Then more pin-
ning, more Sharpie marks, and again the dress was
disassembled. The patterns were refined and passed
on to a "stitcher," who cut and assembled them
with the red linen. Then another fitting, followed by
alterations.

Scott Rött, APT's costume director, told me his
staff does not "make clothes," they "build costumes."
The difference is pronounced at an outdoor theater.
The bodice of Beatrice's dress was lined with cotton
coutil, to minimize wear on the linen—the dress
would be worn 30 times within 5 months—and absorb perspiration that might escape Madden's cami-
sole and corset. Washable dress shields are standard

equipment, of course; some shows are played in full sun and 90-degree heat.

Where a dressmaker might put delicate buttons or no fasteners at all, Beatrice's bodice was equipped with heavy metal snaps, large zippers, and pull tabs to help the backstage dressers get it on and off in a hurry. The skirt was lined with sheer organza, so the hem could be sewn to the lining rather than to the linen itself. It was sewn by hand, not machine, so it could be knotted every ten stitches: if the hem catches on something, only a short stretch of it will pull out. The hem was made with a generous four-inch "seam allowance" to make the skirt easily alterable and adaptable for future use. The bottom was reinforced with a hem protector, since the dress would touch the gritty floor and be dragged through dirt and gravel backstage. The six-page summary of "costume standards" that APT presents to new seamstresses advises, "hem edges that touch the floor will get eaten away during the course of a season. . . . Don't use taffeta or similar 'rustle-y' fabrics, as those fabrics will make a noticeable noise on our stage and DON'T hold up." The hem protector need not be a perfect color match, the standards say. This is one of many instances in which the designers can take advantage of the distance between audience and stage. "If only 1/4" is allowed to show on the right side of the skirt [the side that shows], it will read as a shadow line."

Rött tells me that Beatrice's red dress was one of 46 costumes used in *Much Ado*. Although many were assembled from pieces rented, purchased, made by outside tailors, or rummaged from the company's 36-year stock, five other women's dresses were built from scratch; two of those were made from material that had to be stripped and dyed before construction. One costume was originally built as a wedding dress for a production of *The Taming of the Shrew*. Dyed pink, it reappeared in the 2013 production of *Les Liaisons Dangereuses*. With new sleeves and a few other alterations, it became the dress that Hero wears when Don Pedro, masked and posing as Claudio, draws her aside in the act 2 ball. "Speak low, if you speak love."

THE DAVID FRANK RULES

Actors who were at APT in David Frank's early years recall having the same contradictory feelings that David Daniel had when he first met Frank at Delaware: they didn't fully understand what he was talking about, but he was so passionate and enthusiastic they were pretty sure they needed to figure it out. And they did figure it out, over the years, the director and the actors together, so that now the company has an identifiable Shakespeare aesthetic and a vocabulary to describe it. The veteran actors talk with almost a single voice about things like "Shakespeare time" and "letting the metaphor do the work."

Shakespeare time is a reflection of Frank's passion for poetry—a way to savor language that other directors might cut. "There is an imaginative gen-

erosity in many of Shakespeare's scripts," wrote the
scholar Stephen Greenblatt, "as if he were deliberately offering his fellow actors more than they could
use on any one occasion and hence giving them
abundant materials with which to reconceive and
revivify each play again and again, as they or their
audiences liked it." In other words, the playwright
not only accepted and expected cuts, he provided
cuttable material. Two examples occur in 3.1, the
second gulling scene, as Hero plots with Margaret
and Ursula, her gentlewomen-in-waiting. Their
plan is to bamboozle Beatrice into believing that
Benedick loves her insanely. Hero and Ursula will
walk in the orchard gossiping about his infatuation.
Margaret's task is to fetch Beatrice there so she can
"overhear" the conversation. Tell her to hide here,
Hero says, in the bushes:

> . . . bid her steal into the pleached bower
> Where honeysuckles, ripened by the sun,
> Forbid the sun to enter—like favourites
> Made proud by princes, that advance their pride
> Against the power that bred it.

The context is all scheming: tell Beatrice you
heard us talking about her, get her to hide here,
I'll say this, Ursula will say that. But Shakespeare
interrupts the program for a few words about honey-
suckles blocking the sun and courtiers turning on

their sponsors. Maybe he was referring to Don John the bastard; maybe he had in mind a scandal that his audience would have known about. Maybe both. In any case he was not moving the story forward. He was digressing.

Moments later Beatrice steals onto the stage, and Shakespeare digresses again.

> **Hero:** Now begin,
> For look where Beatrice like a lapwing runs
> Close by the ground to hear our conference.
> **Ursula:** The pleasant'st angling is to see the fish
> Cut with her golden oars the silver stream
> And greedily devour the treacherous bait.
> So angle we for Beatrice, who even now
> Is couched in the woodbine coverture.

A director, particularly one has who never fished a clear trout stream, might be tempted to trim Ursula's fanciful little speech—move things along, get to the funny business. An actor might be inclined to hurry through it. But to Frank, lines like that are half the point. Don't short-shrift that fish, he would say, hold the image up and give the audience a good look. No need to worry about momentum. Just slip into Shakespeare time—a dimension where plot and action and the laws of physics are suspended so that poetry might come forth. If you do it right and give the verse its due, the audience will come with you, and when the poetry is done they'll return with you to the action without missing a beat.

"Let the metaphor do the work" is another way of saying give the words their due. Those words come from one of our greatest writers; they will work if you stay out of their way and let them.

An inept or inexperienced actor might read a speech like Ursula's and play the emotion behind the words rather than the words themselves. Frank wants his Ursula to play the emotion—he wants to hear in her voice and see in her body language the guilty pleasure she's taking in this little conspiracy—but he wants the poetry on top of that. If the actor rushes through the words because she's concentrating too much on looking guilty and conspiratorial, the audience will not see the gift that Shakespeare has given them. The fish cuts the silver stream with golden oars. It's a picture. Paint it.

—

Another of Frank's rules is embodied in his definition of "slow." Before Benedick agrees to challenge Claudio, he and Beatrice have their quarrel:

> **Benedick:** Come, bid me do anything for thee.
> **Beatrice:** Kill Claudio.
> **Benedick:** Ha! Not for the wide world.
> **Beatrice:** You kill me to deny it. Farewell.

Benedick: Tarry, sweet Beatrice.

Beatrice: I am gone though I am here: There is no love in you. — Nay, I pray you, let me go.

Benedick: Beatrice.

Beatrice: In faith, I will go.

Benedick: We'll be friends first.

Beatrice: You dare easier be friends with me than fight with mine enemy.

Benedick: Is Claudio thine enemy?

Beatrice: Is (he) not approved in the height a villain, that hath slandered, scorned, dishonoured my kinswoman? O that I were a man! What, bear her in hand until they come to take hands, and then with public accusation, uncovered slander, unmitigated rancour—O God that I were a man! I would eat his heart in the market place.

Benedick: Hear me, Beatrice.

Beatrice: Talk with a man out at a window! A proper saying!

Benedick: Nay, but, Beatrice.

Beatrice: Sweet Hero, she is wronged, she is slandered, she is undone.

Benedick: Beat—

Beatrice: Princes and counties! Surely a princely testimony, a goodly count, Count Comfit, a sweet gallant, surely. O that I were a man for his sake! Or that I had any friend would be a man for my sake! But manhood is melted into courtesies, valour into compliment, and men are only turned into tongue, and trim ones, too. He is now as valiant as Hercules that only tells a lie and swears it. I cannot be a man with wishing, therefore I will die a woman with grieving.

Benedick: Tarry, good Beatrice. By this hand, I love thee.

Beatrice: Use it for my love some other way than swearing by it.

An actress could deduce that her job in this speech is to convey that Beatrice is angry. But Frank would point out that this exchange goes on for almost 40 lines. How long will it take for the audience to get that Beatrice is angry? And if that's all you're telling them, what reason do they have to keep paying attention? "When the audience knows what's going to happen before it happens," Frank often says, "that's the very definition of 'slow.'"

To put it another way—and he often does—if anger is the only message, what are all those words for?

Look closer at the lines, he would say. She's disappointed: "There is no love in you." Then incredulous at Benedick's dull-witted reaction: "You dare easier be friends with me than fight with mine enemy." She presents her evidence: "slandered, scorned, dishonoured my kinswoman." Erupts into anger: "O God that I were a man!" Presents more evidence: "bear her in hand until they come to take hands." Erupts again: "I would eat his heart in the market place." Turns sarcastic: "Talk with a man out at a window!" Then woeful: "she is wronged, she is slandered, she is undone." Sarcastic again: "Surely a princely testimony, a goodly count, Count Comfit." Then reflective of the sad state of manhood: "But manhood is melted into courtesies, valour into compliment." Each one of these moods, or "colors," as Frank sometimes calls them, is an opportunity to keep the speech aloft, change direction slightly, demand the audience's continued attention. If Beatrice starts angry and just gets angrier for 40 lines, the audience will tune her out. They'll know what's coming. The definition of slow.

"Everybody says they're working on language," Daniel told me. "You won't find a Shakespeare theater that doesn't say they are working on language. But David is the one who doesn't *stop* working on it. At the expense of other things. A lot of directors will say yes, that's important. But when you look at the amount of time they will spend working on a particular line or speech and what David spends working on that line or speech—that's the difference. David doesn't let go of it." He scrutinizes the text for every little turn, every shade of feeling, every minute change of subject. And if after a week or two of rehearsal he doesn't hear them in an actor's speech, he'll halt the proceedings and make a suggestion. *As we go along I'm sure you'll discover that there's a tiny reversal in that line. I mean, if you find it useful. It's for you to decide. No need to go that way, of course, it's just what pops into my head at the moment . . .*

IN THE MOMENT

James DeVita is one of APT's best-known actors. He came to the company in 1995 with his wife, Brenda, who was also an actor then and is now the company's artistic director. In 2014 he directed APT's production of *Romeo and Juliet*. At a preseason presentation for theater supporters and friends, he got a huge laugh with this story:

"*Romeo and Juliet* is actually why I'm at APT; it's why I'm here talking to you right now. Twenty years ago we were working in Chicago—well, *living* in Chicago: Brenda was working; I was auditioning." After five years of actors' marriage—conflicting schedules and long absences—the DeVitas had agreed that whoever got the next offer would take it, and the other would come along. "I got a call from a friend of mine, a colleague, Mr. Ken Albers, who asked me would I be interested in doing Romeo in *Romeo and Juliet*, at this place called APT. So of course I said yes, and we never went back.

"I was not particularly successful in the early parts of rehearsal. I remember Ken telling me that I was the most jaded Romeo he had ever seen. One day he stopped rehearsal, or there was a break, I forget, and Ken calls me over to whisper. You know, the whispering notes from a director are very important—they take you aside from the rest of the cast. So Ken calls me over and I knew it was something big, because usually Ken humiliates me in public. He said come here, as only Ken can do, and he said, umhhh, emhhh, Jim:

"Romeo hasn't read the play. He doesn't know he's in a tragedy."

This story helped me grasp what may be the most common adage of theater, the oft-repeated (and just as oft-forgotten) injunction to be *in the moment*. It's the essential paradox of acting: after reading a speech dozens if not hundreds of times, and committing it to memory, an actor must make it seem as though he is putting it together on the spot; it's coming from his brain as he speaks it.

David Frank sometimes expressed this idea in terms of "reporting" and "discovering." In *Much Ado* 2.2, Don John's servant Borachio tells his master that he can undo the upcoming marriage by staging a scene with Margaret at Hero's bedroom window:

Go, then. Find me a meet hour to draw Don Pedro
and the Count Claudio alone. Tell them that
you know that Hero loves me. Intend a kind of
zeal both to the Prince and Claudio as in love of
your brother's honour who hath made this match,
and his friend's reputation who is thus like to be
cozened with the semblance of a maid, that you
have discovered thus. They will scarcely believe
this without trial. Offer them instances, which
shall bear no less likelihood than to see me at her
chamber-window, hear me call Margaret Hero,
hear Margaret term me Borachio. And bring them
to see this the very night before the intended
wedding, for in the mean time I will so fashion the
matter that Hero shall be absent, and there shall
appear such seeming truth of Hero's disloyalty
that jealousy shall be called assurance, and all the
preparation overthrown.

An actor "reporting" this speech would deliver
it fully baked—as though Borachio had formulated
the whole plan offstage somewhere and was now
presenting it to his master. What Frank wanted
instead was for Marcus Truschinski, the actor who
played Borachio, to "discover" the plan as he spoke,
to make it up as he went along—which not only
would be truer to normal speech and behavior, but
would also better hold the audience's attention.
According to his definition of "slow," the last thing

Frank wants is for the audience to know what's coming. They can't know what Borachio is going to say if Borachio doesn't know himself. Of course Marcus Truschinski knows. His challenge is to forget what he knows as Marcus and stick to what Borachio knows as he speaks—in the moment.

WIG ROOM

———

In the wig room, they love Beyoncé and Dolly Parton—two very public figures who wear wigs and don't care who knows it. Becky Scott, APT's wigmaster, told me a story that she heard from a colleague: "Somebody was taking a tour of Dollywood, and you know Dolly is very accessible when she's there, and someone said oh Miss Parton you're so beautiful, how long does it take to do your hair? And Dolly said well thank you honey, but I don't know 'cause I'm never around when they do it."

That's why APT needs three wigmakers in season. *Much Ado* alone has nearly 30 characters, all of whom need to look like Sicilians of the mid-1800s. Many of the actors in lesser roles can get by with their everyday hair, but Beatrice and Hero have to be done up like aristocrats, as do some of the older male characters, who were designed with elaborate facial hair and flowing white manes. It would take at least a couple of hairdressers to clean, trim, and style all those heads before every show; to do it within the "half-hour," the pre-show call allowed by the Actors' Equity contract, it would probably take a dozen. Hair is more manageable, you might say, if it can be removed from the actors' heads.

Thus the wig room, a quiet alcove off the costume shop. Because of the location and the nature of the work, this is one of the few craft areas at APT where chitchat is possible. The women who work here, hunching close over heads made of plastic foam or canvas-covered cork, seem to have an easygoing rapport, and they arrange themselves in order of volubility. Closest to the door, in good position to entertain visitors and schmooze passing staffers, sits Lara Dalbey, who in APT's off-season is the wigmaster and sole wigmaker at the Milwaukee Repertory Theater. In the middle of the room is the nominal boss, Scott, who will chime in to affirm, amplify, or clarify Dalbey's commentary as necessary; she spends her winters as one of two wigmakers at the Virginia Opera. Back in the corner is Maria Davis, who is sometimes so still and quiet as to become invisible; when not working at APT she's one of a three-person wig staff at the Denver Center Theatre Company.

Their work has a highfalutin name—"ventilating,"

for reasons that remain mysterious to me, and to them—but they usually call it tying or knotting instead. Basically it's a matter of attaching hairs to a nylon mesh, or "lace," that they spread over those inert heads. The open squares of this mesh may be smaller or larger depending on how fine the result needs to be. An intimate indoor theater might require a finer lace than a large outdoor stage; the forehead part of a wig usually needs to be finer than the back.

To build a wig, as they say, the wigmaker holds a loop of hairs in one hand—at APT they use mostly human hair—and a "ventilating needle" in the other. The needle fits into a handle; altogether the tool is about four inches long. The wigmaker dips the end of her needle under the plastic mesh, through one square, and pokes it out again through an adjacent square. The needle's tip is barbed, which allows her now to pick from her other hand a few hairs—or a couple, or one, depending again on the desired result—which she knots onto the nylon with a quick flurry of wrist movements. Then she pulls the needle and hair toward the back of the head, smooths the hair into place, disengages the needle, and dips again. I watched Dalbey and counted about 10 knots in 50 seconds, but she was talking at the same time so she could probably go faster if she needed to.

My guess is that wig-room conversation covers

a wide range of topics. While I was there it was mostly shop talk meant to teach me about the craft.

Dalbey: It's not a difficult thing to do, but you do have to practice at it, you have to get your rhythm down, you have to have an eye for spatial filling. Because that's part of it too, you can't just fill every little hole; people's hair doesn't grow like that. A lot of times the new people I work with just do this so much [getting in real close], because it is really fine work, but they forget to step back. They think, I've got to fill every hole. No you don't, you have to look at how human hair is, how somebody's hairline is. It needs to be more organic.

Scott: That's where instinct comes in. You learn how to do this, you practice it, you work at your knot tying, but when it comes to building a wig with three to five colors, it all comes down to instinct, and learning how to light hair so it looks natural. It also depends on what you're tying. Are you tying intentional highlights in? Do you want somebody to look like they have big chunky highlights? Or do you want it to look more natural? I think this one has three different colors in it. And you can see that there's little streaks of blond in there. But hopefully once this is up in an actual do, when you get it onstage, it will just look natural.

—

Dalbey: There's a generation of directors who think they hate wigs, but what they really hate is bad wigs. That's something that we have to fight against all the time, the director coming in and saying oh, I hate wigs, I don't want anybody wigged, can't we use their own hair? And you just don't understand the consequences of that, the time commitment. If it's a big show there's too many people getting dressed for them to be hairdressing as well.

—

Dalbey: Most of the hair we use in this country comes from India or Asia, and that's because the shaft of dark hair is stronger physically than what we would call European hair. Because the hair is stronger, they're able to take all the color out and then put colors in, so you can get a variety of colors. Depending on what you need for your character. European hair is incredibly expensive. It's hard these days to get a really good white, one that's not yellow or not too gold. Because you can only take dark hair so light before it disappears. If you wanted a white-white, I think you would have to go into a European hair to get that.

Scott: It's expensive. And sometimes you can't use it. The stuff that I built Tracy's wig from last year was stuff that I had to process. [Tracy Michelle Arnold wore a white wig in the company's 2013 production of *Too Many Husbands*.] It was just yellow.

Dalbey: And then we had to bleach it. Becky bleached it. And that's really tricky because if something goes wrong it just turns into mush.
Scott: It just breaks. You can't do anything with it.
Dalbey: A lot of times suppliers say oh yeah, we have white hair, but it's yak hair. And the texture of yak hair, even though you can take it to as white as possible, the texture is Santa Claus. I mean a lot of people use it for Santa Claus. It's real stiff and it's wiry and it's thick.
Scott: Every time you wash it it's got a smell to it.
Dalbey: It's like tying with wire sometimes.
Scott: Oh, yeah. I built a yak hair wig a couple years ago that we dyed two different shades of orange and red, and then permed.
Dalbey: Oh wow.
Scott: And it *still* smells like a wet yak.

—

Dalbey: At Milwaukee Rep I use mostly synthetic hair, and the reason why is once a synthetic wig is set, it stays in that set. Since I don't have a specific wig person who runs shows there, I have to train the wardrobe people to maintain the wigs, and it's just easier to maintain that synthetic wig. They've really come a far way with making that synthetic fiber—and it's funny, 'cause it's actually a trickle-down from the fiber optic industry. They're able to actually make a fiber that is more like hair than just plastic. Thicker at the root and thinner at the bottom. And so it depends. It's hard to pull off blond synthetics, because they reflect light; if you have a blond synthetic onstage and they're under green light it's just awful.

Reporter: So why not use synthetic hair here at APT?

Scott: It doesn't hold up in the sunlight. And the rain.

Dalbey: And bug spray.

Scott: And bug spray.

Dalbey: And synthetic is plastic, and it gets so hot up on that stage it will frizz it out.

—

Dalbey: Sometimes hair is so brittle, especially if you're doing like one hair at a time, you tie it tight and it just snaps. That's usually when it's time to stop and walk away. If you've tied like five knots in a row and nothing stuck, you've got to walk away for a bit. 'Cause you lost your mojo.

Scott: You lost your mojo or you lost your good angle.

Dalbey: Yeah. I think that a good 75 percent of ventilating is the position you're in. And everybody's different. I like the stand. [She had her foam head mounted on a floor stand.] Maria and Becky like to do it in their lap or on the table. In my youth I would do it in my lap, but I can't bend like

that anymore. I can't see that well anymore either;
it's too far away.

—

Scott: I'm trying to break in a new needle . . .
Dalbey: Arghhhh . . .
Scott: . . . and it's got a slightly different angle than
I'm used to. I hate this needle. For the first week
you have a new needle and you're trying to figure
out how that angle is going to work, it's the worst.
Dalbey: We're expecting an order of needles from
a company that we order from in London. And
they just sent the order out. Do we have any more
size 2s, Becky?
Scott: Nope.
Dalbey: Becky broke hers.
Scott: I was here by myself one night, I sat down
with the wig in my lap, tied five knots, my handle
went flying out of my hand, fell on the floor, and
shattered my needle. And it was the last size 2.
Dalbey: Uhhhh.
Scott: I had to go into Lara's stuff and borrow her
size 2 needle because I had none.
Reporter: Is that allowed?
Dalbey: Yes, absolutely, because you know the pain
when you get a needle that you really love. When
that needle breaks, it's like—ohhhhh.
Scott: And that number 2 you have is beautiful.
Dalbey: Thank you.

—

Dalbey [working on a set of sideburns for Leonato]: This is like fronting lace, so it's really fine, because you want to not see the lace for facial hair. These are going to be big chops. Muttonchops. I like making facial hair, beards and things. I look at facial hair on people a lot. There are so many different colors in it. And then you know too, if people are smokers, or when I make a big beard, it kind of fades out at the end—it's pretty amazing.

Maria Davis: Did you guys see the video of the woman making her eyebrows?

Dalbey: No.

Davis: 'Cause that's like the newest trend.

Dalbey: Ventilated eyebrows? Why is it a trend?

Scott: I don't know.

Dalbey: People overtweeze?

Scott: Probably. Well, if you're like a drag queen, you know . . .

Dalbey: Well Whoopi Goldberg, when she does a film, depending on the film, she's got eyebrows.

Davis: Well she has to; she doesn't have anything.

Dalbey: She has nothing. That bugs me. Do you know who else doesn't have eyebrows that bugs the hell out of me? Tony Goldwyn, the president on *Scandal*, if you look at him it's just like—

Scott: Every time I get an opera singer with great eyebrows I always tell them that. You have such a perfect brow shape—they say oh really! I say yeah, because you have no idea how hard it is to put eyebrows on somebody and not make them look quizzical! Or surprised!

Dalbey: I have a tendency to make them look Star Trek usually. Heavy influence of Spock in my life.

—

Dalbey: Sometimes it helps when you call the hair names.

Reporter: Oh yeah? What's that one's name?

Dalbey: Whore, at the moment.

BOSS OF BOSSES

David Frank had the last word. After all the actors tried their bits and all the designers had their say, the set looked like Frank wanted it to look, the music cues came and went where he wanted them to go, and the lines were spoken the way he wanted them spoken, or at least in a way he accepted. Though he was not at all bossy, he was the boss, and not incidentally the head of the company.

But during rehearsals Frank took his orders from Evelyn Matten. She told him where to go, when to show up, and what scene he would be working on next. At the daily break—typically a two-hour period starting in late afternoon—she told him whether he should go to his office to study a scene or go home to take a nap, in which case she phoned to wake him up. She told him when he needed to email the composer, reread a scene, decide on a prop—or have something to eat, put on his sunscreen, or drink some water. Maybe he had room in his head for all this and the whole play too, but Matten wasn't taking any chances.

She was the stage manager of this production, and the head stage manager of the company. Before meeting her I imagined that "stage managers" managed the stage somehow—supervised the stagehands, the changing of sets, the deployment of props, something like that. But the stage is just the end of the job. Matten was the logistical brains of the operation. She was the first to arrive each day and the last to go home. She made the schedules and saw virtually every minute of rehearsal and every performance of the play. She knew about every problem and kept abreast of every solution. While the director and actors and designers and craftspeople tended to their pieces of the show, Matten managed the whole big thing. I came to think of her as the boss of bosses.

From time to time as rehearsals progressed, I sensed the existence of a communication system that was invisible to me. One day someone would express a need for some prop or article of clothing—a box for the gloves that Hero admires on her wedding day, a snuff-stained handkerchief for Don John—and the next day the item would appear. The props or costume people had obviously been involved, but how? A late-night phone call? A hallway conversation? The answer, I eventually learned, was stage management: after every rehearsal, Matten and/or her assistant, Olivia Bedard, prepared a report that was circulated by email to everyone involved in the production: what was rehearsed, who was there, how long they worked, what changes if any were made in the script, and whatever else the costumes, props, lighting, and sound people needed to know. That's how the word went out: Don John needs a hankie. And it was done.

Matten told me that the stage manager is commonly described as the hub of a wheel. "Information passes through us; we disseminate it and stay in touch with the director and the actors and the scene shops. Everybody's working and we're helping it all come together."

She was also the main author and keeper of "the book," sometimes called the production book or the prompt book, a very fat looseleaf binder that, more than any other record or object, embodied the production that was being created. It contained the script, of course, marked up to indicate exits and entrances, lighting changes (yellow tabs), music cues (blue), and much more. It had photos of the backstage prop tables, so the crew would know just where to place and find every prop. It had a "magic sheet" showing the location and specs of 199 stage lights. It had a three-page "run sheet," telling the backstage crew when and where to hand off props, help actors with costume changes, and shine flashlights in the wings for entrances and exits. It had blocking notes showing the location and movement of the actors for each scene—sometimes in diagram form, drawn on an outline of the stage as seen from above, sometimes in handwritten notes. As the show developed and scenes solidified, Matten marked the script with numbers, which corresponded to numbered lines on the facing page of the book; on some of these lines she described the actors' movements with her personal version of stage manager shorthand:

> **Beatrice:** (1) It is a man's office (2) but not yours. (3)
> **Benedick:** (5) I do love nothing in the world so well as you. Is not that strange? (9)
> 1. BEA LK @
> 2. BEN STR ↓, BEA TRN AWAY
> 3. BEA $ A4 SIT - SL
> 5. BEN X, $ A4 SIT - SR
> 9. BEA LK ↑

(1. Beatrice looks at Benedick.) Beatrice: "It is a man's office . . ." (2. He comes down the stairs toward her; Beatrice turns away) "but not yours." (3. She sits on the stage left side of the aisle 4 sittable.) (5. Benedick crosses and sits on the stage right side of the aisle 4 sittable.) Benedick: "I do love nothing in this world so well as you. Is not that strange?" (9. Beatrice looks up.)

One of the purposes of the book, Matten told

TWO PROBLEMS

———

Problems popped up in almost every rehearsal. One might even say that the purpose of rehearsing was to uncover problems and find their solutions. Each problem represented an opportunity to put some flesh on the bare bones of Shakespeare's words. Here are two examples of a process that happened many times:

Act 1, scene 2. Having welcomed the soldiers into his home, Leonato is busy preparing for tonight's ball. House servants scurry around him carrying provisions, arranging the room, placing lanterns. In comes Antonio, Leonato's big brother, with an urgent bit of misinformation.

> **Antonio:** . . . brother, I can tell you strange news that you yet dreamt not of.

Leonato: Are they good?
Antonio: As the event stamps them. (Time will tell.) But they have a good cover, they show well outward. The Prince and Count Claudio, walking in a thick-pleached alley in mine orchard, were thus much overheard by a man of mine: the Prince discovered to Claudio that he loved my niece, your daughter, and meant to acknowledge it this night in a dance . . .

Early in rehearsal, David Frank laid a bit of story on this scene: as Antonio begins to speak, a servant comes in from the wings. Antonio stops and glares at her—she has no business here; he is discussing a matter that's above her station. She catches herself and retreats, embarrassed, uttering a quiet "oops" as she goes.

The purpose of this bit was thematic, I assumed: it said something about the social strata of the household, one of many details meant to add texture to the story. But Anne Thompson, who played the servant (and ad-libbed the "oops"), later told me it also served a technical purpose that in her mind was more important: it underlined Antonio's speech, alerting the audience that something significant was about to be said.

The bit played well and everyone seemed happy with it, but shortly before previews began Thompson discovered a problem: she no longer remembered, if she ever knew, why her character was entering the room.

Oh, we can fix that, Frank said. And in short order he did: Thompson, one of the busy servants seen before Antonio's entrance, would be carrying a lantern. Just before Antonio came on, Tim Gittings, playing a sort of senior servant, would approach and have a word with her, as though he needed her to tend to something. She would nod, set the lantern down, and hurry off to take care of the matter. Then as Antonio began to speak, she would come back in to retrieve the lantern she had left behind, intruding on the gentlemen's confidential conversation.

If she weren't intent on fetching that lantern, Thompson told me, or didn't have some other reason for coming back, her character would go empty for an instant. "It's almost as if the character falls away. Like her existence stops for a second. If I don't know what I'm doing, then I'm going to feel like an impostor out there, and you're probably going to see an impostor. That moment of confusion becomes Anne being confused, as opposed to the character being confused. And I think an audience can more than see that; I think an audience can *feel* that. They can feel a shift in energy and they go, *something was weird about that.*"

Act 3, scene 4. It's almost time for the wedding. We're in Hero's room (evidently—Shakespeare doesn't say) as she speaks with her gentlewoman

Margaret. The dialogue is difficult: prenuptial girl talk, full of indecipherable Elizabethan innuendo. But it clearly establishes that Hero is modest and innocent, while Margaret is neither; that Hero is on edge and Margaret is playful; and that Hero and Margaret are not quite but almost social equals. Margaret feels free to speak her mind on matters of sex and marriage. Hero occasionally upbraids her for doing so, but (unlike the men, who are always escalating their barracks banter) the women quickly reconcile by backing off and shifting to a harmless topic.

Early in the scene Margaret volunteers some fashion advice, prompting Hero to snap at her and insult Beatrice, who is not yet in the room:

> **Margaret:** Troth, I think your other rebato were better.
> **Hero:** No, pray thee, good Meg, I'll wear this.
> **Margaret:** By my troth, 's not so good, and I warrant your cousin will say so.
> **Hero:** My cousin's a fool, and thou art another: I'll wear none but this.

The rebato was a problem. For one thing, many in the audience would not know the word. (It's a stiff ruffled collar of the sort Queen Elizabeth I wears in portraits.) And though it may have been fashionable bridal attire in Shakespeare's time, nobody was wearing them in mid-19th-century Sicily. Bob Morgan had imagined an intimate scene, just us girls in the boudoir. He pictured Margaret in corset and petticoats and Hero in a nightgown and shawl. Still, the rebato remained in the script until the third week of rehearsal, when the actors put the scene on its feet. Then it became apparent that it would have to go.

At this stage in the process, the actors were adding a new dimension to the scene. They had Shakespeare's words; they had Morgan's look. It was up to them now—the actors—to add the action: What are the characters *doing* as they talk? Since that had to match up with what they were saying, adding that third dimension sometimes exposed problems that hadn't been apparent earlier.

Cristina Panfilio, who played Margaret, later recalled: "I think the women in the room imagined that we were dressing Hero for her wedding—because of the nature of the conversation, and also because that would lend an immediacy to our storytelling." So when Hero says "I'll wear none but this," she must be holding or wearing or indicating something. If it's not a rebato, what is it? Her wedding dress? What would that imply for the action? Is she holding up a bulky gown? Does Margaret help her into it as they speak? How would you do that onstage?

Fortunately, Morgan and Jason Orlenko, the

assistant costume designer, were available for an impromptu conference. Orlenko suggested turning the rebato into a veil. Frank assented and Evelyn Matten recorded the script change in her book. The line became "Troth, I think your other veil were better." And that change opened the way for another, as it became clear that the scene would work best with Hero in her wedding dress instead of a nightgown. Margaret could still "dress" her by helping with the finishing touches—her necklace, her gloves, her veil.

The actors grabbed it and ran. When the rehearsal resumed they began fussing with an imaginary veil. No one suggested this fussing; it wasn't planned or discussed; they fell into it naturally and improvised as if by telepathy. Panfilio held up the invisible veil and eyed it critically. "Troth, I think your other veil were better." Kelsey Brennan took it from her and put it on her head. "I'll wear none but this." They walked downstage and stationed themselves in front of an imaginary mirror. Hero primped. Margaret stood behind her and groomed. Looking into the mirror they continued their chatter, which by this time had moved on to a wedding dress worn by the Duchess of Milan.

> **Hero:** Oh, that exceeds, they say.
> **Margaret:** By my troth, 's but a nightgown in respect of yours.

SET BUILDING

━━━

On a hot Friday afternoon at the end of May, I found Bill Duwell out behind the scene shop, wearing a respirator and holding a rectangle of scrap wood that he used as a palette. On it were two globs of paste, one grayish and one reddish, which he mixed together in small amounts with a putty knife. He applied the mixture to a simple wood structure, covering the seams and screw holes to even the surface so the painters could make it look like stone. This was the stage-right sittable, which as rehearsals developed was becoming the locus of three key scenes. Audiences would spend a lot of time looking at it. Duwell said the cosmetic work would go easier if he could use a common wood filler, but he doesn't think fillers stand up to the Wisconsin sun and rain. He prefers Bondo, the legendary stuff of auto body repairs. Bondo has to be mixed on the spot, and the fumes and dust can be toxic. That's why he was out in the sun breathing through a respirator.

Duwell is APT's technical director, the man responsible for getting the sets built, among other things. He reviews the designs, hires the carpenters and metalworkers, watches the budget and safety issues . . . and sometimes, when five sets are being built at once, he puts on the Bondo.

He saw Bob Morgan's set design last November, which was a little earlier than usual. His eye went straight to the trees and his mind started whirring. Would they have to be real and alive? Would they need to be watered? How much does a twelve-foot tree and its ball of roots weigh? How **do** you move it offstage and where do you store it between shows? Maybe the props department could build the trees instead? In November there was no sense overthinking it. Duwell knew the set was likely to change in many ways as the director and designer went back and forth with it. But he made a mental note to follow those trees.

Another thing he noticed right off was the floor, the "stone" patio, which as Morgan had drawn it rose four and a quarter inches over the stage deck. Floors often are drawn that way, Duwell said, because designers assume they will be built on a wood frame of two by fours. Duwell usually tries to persuade them to use a steel frame instead. The steel-frame floors rise only two inches off the deck, which is not enough for some designers and directors, but Duwell knew that David Frank usually prefers the lesser rise. "He feels it plays more like a rug—like the action flows on and off of it better like that." The advantages of the steel frame are that it's lighter and easier for the stage crew to take apart and put together, which they must do for every performance, and it saves storage space, which always looms large in Duwell's mind. At peak season, four sets must be stored in the building behind the main outdoor stage. On average each set needs to fit into about 110 square feet, maybe more if some pieces are light enough to be stored overhead. Designers who are used to doing one show at a time can be rudely surprised by APT's storage needs. Sometimes Duwell takes one look at a set design and knows it will end up being reduced by 40 or 50 percent. Negotiations begin.

As it turned out, Bob Morgan had no quarrel with the short-rise steel frame. And the answer to the tree problem turned out to be plastic. When the set design first came in, Charles "Jen" Trieloff, the prop master, was working at another theater in Arizona. His APT contract covered just four months, May through August. But he was in touch with the year-round staff. He saw the trees and thought he could build them using a trick he had picked up from another props man, something involving glue, horsehair, and paint. But then came March and

APT's "design conference"—a long weekend when directors, designers, composers, choreographers, and the whole season's worth of assorted creative personnel gather in Spring Green to compare notes on the season ahead. There Trieloff learned that Frank wanted the trees to play a role in the lazzi. During his gulling scene, Benedick would be hiding in the trees, poking his head out here and there for comic punctuation. Between pokes, the foliage would have to shake and move convincingly as he stumbled around in it. Trieloff's trees would look great but they wouldn't take to shaking. He wound up buying the trees from a Cleveland company that provides silk flowers and plastic plants for amusement parks and Las Vegas hotels.

—

In April, when *Much Ado*'s set design was all ironed out, Duwell and his assistant, Nate Stuber, figured out how the set would be made and produced detailed drawings for the carpenters to execute. One drawing was devoted to the bottom two steps of the staircase, which were shaped something like lozenges, coming to a point on either side. A caption called them a "Goofy 2 tiered step unit" and went on to specify how it should be built: "Ally wood construction. Mostly .75" aspen with 2×1 nosing trim . . . Glue and screw. Fill and sand. Break all edges for less boot shatter . . ." A note higher up on the page alerted the carpenters that the unit was "Not symmetrical. Because why the fuck would it be, right?"

As I poked around the scene shop, I expected to see a lot of this head-shaking and eye-rolling. Having met a few tradesmen who had zero tolerance, if not outright disdain, for their clients' whims and ignorance—guys who always knew a better way and were always wondering what in the world you'd want to do *that* for—I imagined I'd find some tension between the dreamy artists who designed the show and the practical-minded craftsmen who had to execute their dreams in wood and metal. But I was surprised: the notes on that drawing were the only discouraging words I found. Indeed I was struck by the patience and cheerfulness—the dedication!—with which the manual workers did the artists' bidding.

I asked Duwell about it one day as he drove up the hill from the scene shop to install a new piece on the *Much Ado* set. At the show's first preview, someone had noticed that when David Daniel poked his head out of the trees, he was leaning so far forward that he had to hold onto the trees to keep from falling—not good for the trees and certainly not safe for the actor. The scene shop had been asked to build an extension that would allow Daniel to step another foot or so into the trees. Now it had been built—a wooden box, essentially—and painted to match the faux-stone finish of the set, though it would be invisible to almost the entire audience. As Duwell drove it up the hill he quickly explained the mystery of the agreeable craftsmen.

Most of the people in the company, he told me, had come from theater schools, where nuts and bolts are taught alongside acting and literature. The majority of the carpenters, the electricians, even many of the seamstresses had at least a bachelor's degree from a theater program, and some had more. (Duwell was an exception, but he considered himself an outlier; to get his job today, he said, he'd need an MFA.) So the craftspeople were not ignorant or even skeptical about the importance of artistic details; rather they took their importance for granted. The dress has to button *exactly* here? The music has to sound like it's coming from the living room, not the garden? The leaves have to shake just so? Of course they do. Give the artists what they want. It's all in service of the story. My mistake: where I had expected tradespeople working in the theater, I found theater people working at the trades.

OFF BOOK

━━━

Sunday, June 1: For the first time in four weeks of rehearsal, the pieces of *Much Ado* are strung together into a whole play—the "designer run," a chance for the lighting designer, the composer, the set and costume people, and everyone else to get a sense of how the production is coming together and what problems remain to be solved. From here they'll have a week to finish rough drafts of their work before three nights of "tech" runs, APT's equivalent of dress rehearsals, with sound, lights, costumes, wigs, and props.

Tuesday, June 3: *The Importance of Being Earnest*, which will have its first tech this evening, has primary status for today's afternoon rehearsal block. While that cast works on the big stage, David Daniel and

Colleen Madden confer quietly with David Frank in the rehearsal room. Frank is pleased with the way the Beatrice-Benedick relationship unfolded in the designer run, but he has a bit of advice for Daniel's big moment: "I won't really know this until we're back on the big stage, or perhaps even with an audience—I love the boldness of your choice, David, to declare your love to her with your back to her, I mean I just I love it. I don't want to lose that for all the tea in China, I just think it's so right. You may need a little bit of a head movement or something to tell the audience to concentrate on you. Because they are going to have to concentrate. You may need to find just enough of a weight shift or a head shift, something to alert the audience, because otherwise they're not going to be looking to you to speak. They won't know where to be looking next. And so if you can just give them something so they'll know—*Oh! There's something happening!* We'll learn more about that in front of an audience."

Thursday, June 5: John Tanner, the composer and sound designer, is holed up in a room at the Spring Green Motel, surrounded by computers, speakers, keyboards, and cans of food. Many of the latter are doubling as stands for his two extra-wide flat-screen monitors. With this stuff and a large library of recorded sound samples, Tanner can conjure a symphony orchestra, and that's what he likes to do.

He tells me there are two kinds of theater music. One kind comes from the world of the play—as the characters sing songs, play lutes, or dance to the music of an offstage party band. The other kind comes from God. Tanner prefers to write for God.

He's come to Spring Green from Milwaukee, where with a partner he runs a music and video studio that does advertising work for such brands as Toyota, Hilton, and Sears. In his younger days he was an LA rocker whose closest brush with fame was playing in a band with Warren Zevon and Phil Everly. (This was the mid-70s. The Everly Brothers had gone separate ways and Warren Zevon was not yet Warren Zevon. The band "never played a gig," Tanner told me.) In the 80s he engineered two albums, including a platinum seller, for the Milwaukee rock band Violent Femmes, and through their producer got started doing theater music. He likes researching and immersing himself in various styles and periods. "I don't know how many talents I have," he says, "but I know one: ever since I was young I've been able to listen to something and inhabit its musical world fairly accurately. It's a weird knack. When I was in college, one of our challenges was we had to pick a piece of music and kind of rip it apart, find out what made it tick, and write our own version of it. And that's something I can *do*."

For *Much Ado* Tanner is inhabiting the musical world of Verdi. With the first tech three days away, he has finished writing, orchestrating, and recording music for the prelude, two dances, and two songs that will be sung in the play. Now he's working on the sound cues that will punctuate the performance—music that will start scenes, end them, and provide transition from one to another.

At the end of 2.1, for example, Don Pedro, the matchmaking prince, has just announced his plan to "bring Signor Benedick and the Lady Beatrice into a mountain of affection th'one with th'other. . . . Go in with me," he tells his accomplices, "and I will tell you my drift." As they exit the music is light and comic, oboe and flute, merry and perhaps a bit mischievous. But now the villain Don John and his sidekick Borachio walk on. They are about to concoct the big lie. The music continues, sustains, and shifts seamlessly to a minor key as the underlying pulse becomes more prominent and ominous. It's a microsymphony, about sixteen seconds long. Tanner has 23 of these to finish before Sunday.

He tells me he has been in the motel room for six days now, eating soup and chili, working twelve, sixteen, eighteen hours a day. "This is unbelievable," he says. "This is a ton of music. It's just killing me." It looks to me like he's having a good time.

Friday, June 6: The set is up. Frank walks up the hill and into the amphitheater and stops cold at the sight of it. There are two pedestals on the upper level, each one topped with an obelisk about three feet tall. Frank wanted the set to suggest repressive patriarchy, but this is a little too masculine for him. He has a delicate chat with Bob Morgan, who will later confess that the obelisks were bigger than he wanted them to be—he had drawn them to the wrong scale and the scene shop had built them exactly as ordered. Frank asks the stage crew if the obelisks can come off. Morgan wants a chance to fix them and says removing them "would be a mistake. We lose a huge amount of the design." A stagehand lifts them off and they never come back.

Weeks later Morgan was sanguine about it. "They were part of that thing I was trying to do to make weight and masculinity happen, rather than having round, finial balls. I wanted something more interesting. And I found them in the research. But then I ruined my chance because I made a mistake when I drew them. It was dumb. Just a stupid dumb mistake. It's all fine; it worked out fine."

The actors are all "off book" now. When rehearsals started almost everyone worked with script book in hand. After a week or so they started going scriptless, one actor at a time as each became comfortable doing so. Now they're all trying to say their lines from memory. Sometimes they go blank and abruptly call out "Line," at which point Evelyn Matten or Olivia Bedard instantly feeds them the words. One or the other has to read along with every speech. They cannot get caught up in the acting or let their attention wander.

Jacki Singleton, the stage manager for *American Buffalo*, is here to help today, even though her own show will have a tech rehearsal tonight and a preview tomorrow. (Matten will do the same for *Romeo and Juliet* on Tuesday.) She sits several rows back with a copy of the script and a sheaf of forms. When she hears a mistake she writes the date and time, the actor's name, and a script page number. She can circle one of nine prefab notes on the form and specify the transgression below.

Paraphrased	Dropped	Jumped cue
Inverted	Added	Late on cue
Substituted	Called for line	Check script

You said: _____.
The line is: _____.

At the end of rehearsal she walks about handing out her notes, which the actors accept gratefully. Some come toward her and gather round, reminding me of soldiers at mail call in a 50s war movie.

Sunday, June 8: Today Frank is fine-tuning the beginning of the play, seeing the action in his head, waving his cast of invisible actors on and off stage while the composer and sound technician adjust the volume and timing of the music. When that's done the real actors come on for rehearsal. This is one of two "ten out of twelve" days allowed in the schedule according to the company's Equity contract: normally the cast is on call for eight hours each day, but today they can be called for as many as ten hours in the twelve-hour period between noon and midnight. They rehearse from one till five, take a break, and come back at seven for their first tech run.

Before the tech begins, Morgan's obelisks are replaced—with the round finial balls he was trying to avoid. His set has had a sex change. As soon as the show starts he sees that it also looks too bright—particularly the flowers on the gates and the hats and aprons worn by the servants. If there's too much stark white, he says, people's pupils will shut down and they won't be able to see the actors' faces. "I've worked on comedies where the director kept saying, more light, more light, I can't see!" Morgan has to explain that the answer is not more light but less. The flowers will be painted to tone them down; as for the caps and aprons, "we'll just dunk 'em," he says.

Tuesday, June 10: Another tech is scheduled for this evening. Now it's midafternoon and various scenes are being rehearsed on the set. Most of the cast are present, sitting out in the house when they don't have to be onstage. And as the show has come closer to opening, the number of craftspeople and onlookers has been increasing. It's not an audience, exactly, but a lot more spectators than usual, and Madden is performing for them. She seems to have found a new gear: she's saying her lines more distinctly and meaningfully; her speeches seem to have more corners in them. And the rest of the cast is feeding off her—Brian Mani as Leonato, Kelsey Brennan as Hero, Chris Klopatek as the messenger. They all seem sharper, their characters more alive. Three more days before they get a real audience.

Saturday, June 14: "I think we're on the brink of something very special," Frank says. After two more techs and many hours of smaller rehearsals, last night the company presented the first of two previews for some 760 patrons—an audience at last. Now the whole cast is meeting in the "veranda," a breezy screened-in room behind the main stage. "I was ecstatic with how the audience listened and how well that story played," Frank says. "We've got work to do, we've got actually more than enough time to do it, and it's fun work, finishing work, detail work. I've got a few notes here and there." Six weeks ago he watched rehearsals without saying a thing. Now he's gone granular:

"Tim, Anne, Victoria [household servants], I love having that little household group there. Try not to make it three shoulders in a line. See if you can make it a little triangular pod."

"Eric [Don John], when sitting on the down-left sittable in your first scene, if you could find at least one or maybe a couple moments to share a bit more with house right—just a weight shift, the tiniest; imagine that way as well as that way."

"Colleen, is it possible for you to start the audible sobbing a little earlier?"

He runs through his list and then asks the actors if they have any issues. They discuss the pacing of the second half, the crowd reactions in the aborted wedding, the transition between the two gulling scenes. Then Matten has some news for the gentlemen about the shave chart—it will be up in a few days, she apologizes for the delay, she hopes it will prevent misunderstandings later in the season about who is and who is not allowed to have facial hair. And everyone, please, when you're sitting around the green room at performance time, be judicious about your wifi use. The bandwidth is used by the gift shop's sales system, and stage management might need it to monitor the weather. Please no streaming of music or movies. Bring a book.

After about half an hour the cast is dismissed. Like a speaker hanging around the podium after his talk, Frank chats one-on-one with actors who come to him with questions or worries. Gradually they drift off to their other duties. Since yesterday evening they have been immersed in *Much Ado*, but Kelsey Brennan and Cristina Panfilio have major roles in *Earnest*, which opens tonight at 8. Madden has the first tech of *R&J* tomorrow at 7. Right now she's off to the indoor theater, where her husband, James Ridge, and her *Much Ado* uncle, Brian Mani, will open *American Buffalo* in less than two hours. She departs telling the director that the preview was "really, really fun."

"Good-good," Frank replies. "More-more." Then he and Matten huddle for another half hour, making a list of scenes to work and problems to solve. They have five days before the next preview, seven days till opening night.

RAIN DELAY

―――――

After its first preview, *Much Ado* had to yield the big stage to the opening of *Earnest* and three nights of tech for *R&J*. The cast went back to rehearsing the show in bits and pieces, and by the night of their second preview, Thursday, June 19, they had just about forgotten the experience of performing for an audience. Spirits were high that afternoon. In the backstage men's room I conducted an impromptu standing interview with Tim Gittings, who played two roles in the show: at the beginning and end he was a nameless house servant; in the middle he was Verges, the sidekick of Dogberry, the constable in charge of the Watch. I was unable to take notes or operate a recorder during this interview, so the following is from memory:

Reporter: Everyone seems to be up today. It's a happy day. Is that because there's an audience tonight, or you're all starting to feel like the show is done, or what?

Gittings: Yeah, it's a couple of things. People are getting comfortable with where the show is at. There are a few things left to polish, but eventually you get to the point where you need an audience to make it better and drive new changes. So having an audience tonight is exciting.

The company's enthusiasm was soon dampened. About 6 p.m. it began to rain. Not a drizzle or an afternoon thunderstorm but a steady rain that looked like it would last till morning. The sky was thick and gray in every direction.

The audience was not deterred. At 7 there were hundreds of cars in the parking lot and a stream of theatergoers ascending the hill in a winding procession. Many were under umbrellas; some wore plastic ponchos; one guy was stripped down to shorts and sneakers. It was an impressive display of devotion, and experience. The audience knew that the bleakest-looking weather could change quickly; many of them had seen shows completed in circumstances that looked just as bad. They also knew the rain rules: the company would perform in a light rain if they could, would hold the show for as long as 45 minutes, and would issue refunds only if the performance was canceled before intermission. (If canceled later, tickets could be exchanged but not refunded.) They had paid as much as $58 for those tickets. Many had driven a long way. They loved their theater. Up the hill they went.

Show time, 7:30, came and went and the rain continued. The cast waited calmly in the green room behind the stage. Those who would appear in the first scene, if there was one, were costumed, coiffed, and ready for action. But a few who would not appear until after intermission were half dressed or still in street clothes. They sat on a long couch, a motley and incongruous group swapping stories, flipping through magazines, staring at smartphones: a woman in a ridiculously voluminous dress, with a hairdo from another world; a military man in a crisp blue and red uniform with a sword at his side; a teenage boy in T-shirt and jeans; an older gentleman with a top hat and huge white muttonchops. They were used to this.

The audience was too. People squeezed into the gift shop and congregated under the limited shelter provided by the outdoor "lobby." Some waited farther down the hill, near the box office or under a large canopy in the picnic area.

In the tech booth at the back of the house, Evelyn Matten watched the radar on her computer screen and checked in with Bob Lindmeier, the chief meteorologist at Madison's WKOW, channel 27. She wanted badly to get this show in. A rainout can cost the company thousands of dollars—sometimes tens of thousands. More important on this particular evening, the show needed work in front of an audience. This was the last chance to do it before opening night on Saturday. If the weather didn't clear they would try to do the show anyway, inviting the audience to watch in the rain for free.

A little after 8 p.m., David Frank ducked out of the booth and sat at the back of the house to feel the rain for himself. According to the promise APT makes to its patrons, they would have to make a decision by 8:15. The rain had let up a bit, but not enough to play a three-hour show in. Frank went back to the booth and told Matten he thought it was hopeless. They should call it off. OK, Matten said, just let me try Bob Lindmeier one more time.

Lindmeier has been helping APT for years and is quite familiar with the way the weather moves across the Wisconsin River and over the hill. On his equipment, which gave him a more sophisticated picture than Matten could get on the internet, he saw an opening. The front seemed to be dissipating. The rain would stop. The radar showed more rain coming in behind it, but if they started soon they might get to intermission before it arrived. Because of their 45-minute promise, and the anticipated arrival of the second wave of rain, they'd have to begin now, under a soft shower. Could they ask this of their audience? Should they? To go or not to go, that was the question.

Back behind the stage, Jacki Singleton stood at the door of the green room watching over an increasingly restless cast. About 8:15 the phone rang and the room went quiet. Singleton picked up the receiver and listened. *We're going.* The cast cheered softly. The audience was invited to take their seats.

At 8:22 the lights went down and the horn sounded out in the woods. Hero came onto the bridge, followed by Beatrice, and the messenger came looking for Leonato. Leonato appeared and as the two of them hurried off stage left, Brian Mani slipped on the wet deck and his large body went down with a crash. The audience gasped. Frank and Matten, who had decided that the show would go on in the rain, no doubt experienced a brief moment of panic.

"I felt like I skidded two and a half feet," Mani told me the next morning. "And it felt like it took me 30 seconds to fall. *Oh shit oh shit oh shit oh shit—here it goes.* And the first thing that went through my mind as I was falling is I've got to let them know I'm all right. So as soon as I hit I got up on one knee and just put my hand up like I'm fine, I'm fine. Went off, and then I even faked a little limp as I walked in. Because they need to be OK with that before they can hear the play."

Leonato: I learn in this letter . . .

The rain stopped about 9 and never came back. The show played well, under the circumstances. Some of the audience stood at curtain call. Mani had a bruise on his midsection—he had fallen on a large costume medallion—but the only other casualty was a bit of lazzi that David Daniel had planned into his gulling scene. He hides behind the stage-right sittable and, thinking he can't be seen by his comrades, jumps up and moves stage left. After a short time there he jumps up again, speaking an aside as he makes a dash for the trees, and performs a double pratfall, tripping elaborately over the bench and then crashing into the wall, in approximately the same place where Mani took his fall. I'd watched Daniel work on this stunt for weeks in rehearsal, reciting the sequence of moves under his breath: Up, speak, turn, fall, stand, crash. Up, speak, turn, fall, stand, crash. He executed it perfectly that night, but many in the audience thought he had slipped and fallen as Mani had. Where he wanted a big laugh, he got a collective gasp.

PRELUDE

═══════

In the Folio, the cross-stage move that Mani slipped on does not exist. The text begins with this stage instruction: "Enter LEONATO, governor of Messina, HERO his daughter, and BEATRICE his niece, with a messenger." Leonato already has the letter in hand.

What happened just before? Where are they entering from? What time of day is it? How did Leonato receive the letter? Some directors, if not most, feel free to imagine a prelude before the first line. It's a chance to set the mood, state a theme, or even to inject some information that Shakespeare didn't bother to include. It's like the precredit sequence in a movie. In Joss Whedon's 2012 film version of the play, the prelude is a morning bedroom scene that says explicitly what Shakespeare only hints at, that Beatrice and Benedick share an intimate past. In Kenneth Branagh's version, the song "Sigh No More" is moved to the beginning and recited as a poem by Emma Thompson, whose bronze tan and fabulous hair decorate a scene of bucolic sensuality: Leonato's household and servants are enjoying a picnic on a green hillside; we see many white dresses, bare shoulders, grapes and figs, and much merry laughter at the women's complaint expressed in the song.

In David Frank's version, the prelude sketched the relationship of the main female characters. Hero embodies the virginal anticipation of a house that is about to be filled with amped-up soldiers. She is pretty, innocent, and all aquiver at the promise of distant trumpets. Maybe she has a particular fellow in mind.

Beatrice, by contrast, has been around the block. She knows what's going through her cousin's mind and she's tickled by it. It's foolish, but inevitable and kind of touching.

So the horn sounds. Hero comes out, expectant. Beatrice follows, amused. We learn a little about these characters, and in the course of imparting that information the prelude also performs what may be its most important function at APT. Many performances here start before dark. Lights are useless. The prelude tells the audience: Hush yourselves, stop your squirming, this is it. The play has begun.

OPENING NIGHT

———

Much *Ado* opened on Saturday night, June 21, before an audience of 995, who received it very enthusiastically. "Lovely audience," Evelyn Matten recorded. "Responsive throughout. Standing ovation, almost immediately."

APT and its audience do not make much of "opening night." It's little more than an asterisk on the calendar; tickets prices don't even go up. Mostly it's an internal concept—the night when rehearsals and changes end, the cast has a party, and critics are welcomed in to review the show.

Reviews don't mean as much here as they do at other theaters. I once asked David Frank about the notices he got in his early years as artistic director, and he couldn't remember. When he arrived at the company, he said, "I was kind of accustomed to saying OK, what's the review? What does the *Post-Dispatch* say? What does the *Buffalo News* say? Is it up, down, or halfway? And everything else doesn't matter. Here the reviews were always so disparate, from so many different sources. There wasn't one reviewer. They kind of canceled each other out."

Twenty-four years later the company is regarded as a civic asset and reviews tend to run from mildly to wildly positive. Southern Wisconsin is not the sort of theater market that requires or encourages much negativity. A bad review probably wouldn't deter many theatergoers anyway. A lot of APT's customers are confirmed fans, and many plan their visits before the season starts. The general reputation of the company is much more important than reviews of individual shows. You won't see a lot of quotes about particular plays in the company's publicity or on its website, but you're not likely to escape that Terry Teachout quote about APT being the best classical theater company in America.

Nonetheless, Frank and his company must have been gratified by the published reaction to their show. The critics loved it. More important, perhaps, they saw the show that Frank and his cast wanted them to see—a deeper, more thoughtful *Much Ado* that dealt in ideas and relationships in addition to eavesdropping and mischief. Aaron R. Conklin of *Madison* magazine wrote:

Give Madden and Daniel major credit for capturing the nuances of two people simultaneously scared to death of being forever alone and actually giving their heart to someone else. He wears his wit like a literal suit of armor. She laughs away anything uncomfortable, like swiping at an annoying mosquito.

But the real devil is in the details: It's in the tight-lipped smile Madden strains to hold after Daniel darts away from their conversation. It's in the extra heartbeat or two each allows to hang in the air as they look away uncomfortably toward the audience after an acid-tipped insult or unexpected tender line. It's in the real heat and anger each puts into their verbal attacks once they've been wounded. There's a depth here that isn't always present in more frothy productions of *Much Ado*. Director David Frank's gone for the heart and mind, not the funny bone, and that's a daring and interesting choice.

In Milwaukee's *Journal Sentinel*, Mike Fischer wrote:

For all the frat-boy bluster he shares with his fellow military officers, Daniel's Benedick is as sensitive and insecure a version as you're ever likely to see. Even in the first scene, as Benedick jokes about why he's a confirmed bachelor, Daniel sounds and looks wistful rather than satisfied or sure. This Benedick has wearied of the barracks and their banter. But he hasn't yet figured out how to break free . . .

[Through many strategic choices] Frank amplifies what Madden's Beatrice consistently makes clear: Women in this patriarchal world get a raw deal.

Gwendolyn Rice in *Isthmus*, Madison's alternative weekly:

Madden and Daniel play Beatrice and Benedick as reluctant lovers who use cleverness to cover the hearts they wear on their sleeves. Instead of being merely a foolish braggart, Daniel's Benedick uses his bluster to disguise his earnest affection, woefully unsure of his footing in the arena of love (literally, to great comic effect). Likewise, Madden's Beatrice harbors a deep longing for Benedick in between her sarcastic, scathing lines. Their love story is enormously compelling, in part because of the clumsy, awkward ways they reveal it to each other, encouraged by their friends and family.

Madden and Daniel are masterful in their roles, delivering jibes with breezy intelligence one minute, struggling to cover their insecurity in love the next. . . .That they can each communicate such a wide range of intensity and emotion with a look is simply stunning to watch.

ANOTHER PROBLEM

———

Act 3, scene 2: Claudio and Don Pedro are giving Benedick a hard time. He has shaved his beard, washed his face, and rubbed himself with civet. "Conclude, conclude," crows Pedro, "he is in love." It's a manly display of affection, friendly mockery mixed with macho aggression. As Benedick moves to poke Claudio playfully in the chest, Claudio catches his arm and twists, immobilizing the older soldier without seeming to expend much effort.

This was David Daniel's idea. When he knew he had won the role of Benedick, he began filling a composition book with notes on his lines and character. He does this for every role, he told me. On one page he drew a sword and wrote:

SWORDS

to give the challenge more weight—is it possible to
have fencing play w/Claudio . . . this play sets up
Claudio as the better swordsman and adds tremen-
dous weight to the challenge.

The swordplay never happened, but Daniel and
Nate Burger, the actor who played Claudio, developed the arm-twisting to serve the same purpose.
"DD was playing the long game," Burger told me.
"He needed some fuel for the end of the play. He
wanted it to be clear when Benedick does the challenge to Claudio, that Claudio could physically
best him."

But the bit became a problem, and sometime in
late summer it was gone. "It was hard to do," Burger
recalled. "It required more precision than you'd
think it would need, and we didn't really figure it
out in a real way. We didn't give a lot of time to it
in rehearsal."

Burger was grabbing Daniel's arm without
seeming to look at it. One night he missed, and "it
looked like the fakest thing in the world. It had sort
of been building to that—there was a lot of fum-
bling and physical looseness—and it came to a point
where DD was like, what do we want to do about
this? And I said let's cut it and make it something
different. And he said I love that."

Burger told me he was never wholly comfortable

with the arm-twisting. "I don't know if I was ever sold on it in terms of character, actually. It was playful, but I don't think Claudio *is* that playful. I think he's a dude who's fundamentally governed by his insecurities. He's convinced—*my* Claudio is convinced—that he's the stupidest person in the room, because he's surrounded by these two really charismatic forces, and doesn't have the same sort of sharp wit and quickness that Don Pedro or Benedick have. So it was easy for him to believe that those guys had tricked him and stolen away Hero—like of course man, I should have known, I'm so stupid."

Burger replaced the arm-twisting with a hard stare. "Then it was kind of oh, OK, we're not playing. That was more on point in terms of character for me. So it just became a different thing, and I think we both felt better about it then."

IN THE BOOTH

―――――

Late in July, halfway through the run, I sat with Evelyn Matten and her colleagues in the tech booth behind the audience. It was eerie in there. We watched the actors through panes of glass and heard their voices through a tinny speaker. It was like watching TV; the audience sounded like a laugh track. Being separated from the players like that somehow made me acutely aware of the artifice of the show. I had seen it from the house six or seven times by then and always got swept up in the story. But all I could see from the booth was actors at work. I wondered if Matten ever got to see the show, or any show, the way an audience member would.

To her left in the booth was Eliot Garfield, the company's master electrician, who was operating the lights. To her right was sound apprentice John Leahy, who was running the sound. The lights and sound had been programmed by their respective designers, John Tanner and Michael Peterson; the technicians in the booth were mostly tapping computer keys at Matten's cues, which she announced with one eye on her prompt book and one on stage. The book provided only approximate guidance; because the actors' movements can change from night to night, she cues by what they're doing, not necessarily what they're saying. In the book she had marked not only the cues but also standbys for each cue, indicated by "S/B." Every time she announced a standby, the technician would acknowledge it by saying "Lights" or "Sound." Matten would acknowledge every acknowledgment by saying "Thank you."

> **Friar:** Come lady, die to live. This wedding day perhaps is but prolonged. Have patience and endure.
> **Matten:** Standby lights 77.
> **Garfield:** Lights.
> **Matten:** Thank you.
> **Benedick:** Lady Beatrice, have you wept all this while?
> **Beatrice:** Yea, and I will weep a while longer.
> **Benedick:** I will not desire that.
> **Beatrice:** You have no reason, I do it freely.
> **Benedick:** Surely I do believe your fair cousin is wronged.

Beatrice: Ah, how much might the man deserve of me that would right her!

Benedick: Is there any way to show such friendship? [Beatrice X↓ off stairs]

Matten: Lights 77. Go.

Beatrice: A very even way, but no such friend.

Benedick: May a man do it?

Beatrice: It is a man's office, but not yours.

For a smaller, simpler show in the indoor theater, Matten would generally tap her own keys, but here she needed help. While she called out the sound and light cues, she operated the cue lights by herself. These lights ("Q/L" in the book) are placed backstage and in the woods for actors who can't see or hear what's happening onstage. When the light goes on, they get ready. When the light goes off, they go on. The timing has to be precise.

The night I sat in the booth, the first half of the show ran 1 hour, 16 minutes, 47 seconds by Matten's stopwatch—a little longer than usual, according to the performance reports in the book. During intermission, David Frank dropped in with a few observations. Colleen Madden had asked him to have a look at Beatrice's gulling scene. She was afraid it was getting a little too giddy, but Frank told Matten it was going fine, no problem. He did have a note for David Daniel, however. His Benedick was showing excess facial activity.

Frank could have shared these comments with the actors in his office, or in the parking lot, or in the aisle of the Hometown Supermarket in Spring Green. But generally, Matten told me, after opening night the director gives any notes to the stage manager, and s/he relays them to the cast. At most theaters, directors depart after their shows open, for home or the next job. In some situations their opinions might actually be unwelcome beyond that point. That's not likely at APT, where the atmosphere is more familial than formal, and of course Frank, the head of the company, wasn't going anywhere. But the tradition persists: On opening night the director is done; now the show belongs to the cast and the stage manager.

The second half of the show ran 1:16:35—also about a minute longer than usual. Matten recorded in the performance report that it played to a "small house," 615 people, but that it was a "fun, attentive" audience. She noted the six times they applauded before the end, and that Abbey Siegworth, playing Ursula, may have been having voice problems. "Abbey's voice sounding a bit raspy tonight. Becca L. [another stage manager] reported the possibility of this earlier in the day due to her work in *Doctor's Dilemma*." Also noted: a cell phone rang during 5.1. The whip-poor-will, a summer fixture, started up at 9:03.

BALANCING ACT

David Frank was fond of saying that *Much Ado* is a tragedy wrapped in a comedy. Between the opening badinage and the happy ending dance, a woman is slandered by her fiancé, betrayed and threatened by her father, and left for dead on her wedding day. The best she can hope for, it seems, is to spend her many remaining years in a convent. The night Frank popped into the booth to talk about Beatrice's gulling scene and David Daniel's facial activity, he was indirectly addressing what I came to see as the essential challenge of the show: the balance between the tragedy and the comedy, the gravitas and the laughs.

Over the years APT has developed a loyal audience attentive to an ever-widening range of "classical" theater. But Shakespearean comedies are always the top draw. Not only are they the most familiar shows, they also go best with the other elements of the experience—the picnics, the woods, the wine, the starry summer skies. Audiences come ready to laugh, and the collective desire of a thousand people can exert a powerful pull. Some of the ideas Frank wanted to explore—the confinement of women, the delusion of simple answers, the shallowness of young love and the complications of mature—were in constant tension with the theatergoers' determination to have a good time.

The "Kill Claudio" line was the most poignant instance, but there were others. In early rehearsals, for instance, I thought Frank was trying to develop two quite distinct gulling scenes. On Benedick's side, David Daniel had lots of physical business in mind, and it was clear that he would be playing for big laughs—getting his sleeve or pants leg caught in a fence, for example, and struggling to extricate himself without being noted. But Frank and the actors worked hard to develop a story that Claudio, Leonato, and Don Pedro could play in the foreground. They settled on a tale of nervous amateur thespians warming to their task. They're acting for Benedick's benefit—pretending to have a conversation about Beatrice's crush and pretending not to know that Benedick is overhearing them. As they begin they are incompetent and uncertain, but gradually they become comfortable with their deception and then get caught up in it, until Leonato is gesturing and declaiming as though realizing a lifelong ambition.

On the female side, Frank wanted Beatrice's gulling to show a change in the character of Hero. In the beginning of the play she's just a pretty face: she says almost nothing and seems to go whichever way the men point her. But when she is accused on her wedding day, she must flash anger and stand up for herself against the men, including her father. Frank wanted the gulling scene to mark the beginning of her growth from malleable girl to independent woman. She's in the habit of deferring to her older cousin, and ducking her withering wit. But now Beatrice is hiding in the woodbine coverture and Hero can vent some pent-up feelings, pretending she doesn't know that Beatrice can hear.

> Nature never framed a woman's heart
> Of prouder stuff than that of Beatrice.
> Disdain and scorn ride sparkling in her eyes,
> Misprising what they look on, and her wit
> Values itself so highly that to her
> All matter else seems weak . . .
>
> But who dare tell her so? If I should speak,
> She would mock me into air, O, she would laugh me
> Out of myself, press me to death with wit.

As Kelsey Brennan played it, Hero gathered strength and confidence as this speech went on, upping the ante at several turns until she was standing on the stage-left sittable and letting it all out with glee and relish. Abbey Siegworth's Ursula was so scandalized by this display of gumption that she backed fearfully toward Beatrice's hiding place and spread her dress out like a cape, as though blocking Beatrice's vision might keep her from hearing Hero's tirade.

To my eye (and Colleen Madden's, I believe), the scene played well and made sense in rehearsal, but evidently Frank began to fear that it wasn't funny enough. As comedic business was added in, I thought some nuance was lost. Madden did a bit with the iron gates—inadvertently slamming them at one point, which Hero and Ursula have to pretend not to hear, and later coming out from the alcove and letting the gate close behind her. She tugs and strains and finally pries it open, ducking back inside just before Hero and Ursula pretend not to see her.

The comedy seemed to escalate when the rehearsals moved onto the big stage and the real set, and it got broader still when the audience arrived. I thought Hero's character development survived, but I was looking for it; I wondered if the audience was getting it amid the hilarity. I also thought the two gulling scenes wound up looking too much like parallel versions of the same scene. They even had matching moments: Beatrice forgets herself and giggles at Hero's description of her; Benedick forgets himself and gasps when he hears that Hero might do a desperate outrage to herself; in both cases the gullers have to stifle their laughter, pretending they didn't hear. But David Frank said it was all OK the evening he came into the booth, and he told me the same when the run was over. "I think you're wrong," he said. "I don't think the female scene is anywhere near parallel. I felt it was much more different than most female gulling scenes are. In fact lots of people who know the play and even directors remarked on how it didn't echo, as so often happens.

"There was a moment when Colleen said to me, I'm mourning us taking it totally seriously, and I said no, we need to have both. Because if we don't have any levity to it, it's too long a scene for the content. I'm sure I'm right there. If we had left it as absolutely dead serious as we initially started exploring it, it wouldn't have worked. I'm sorry, I've just been doing this too long. I'm sure of it."

—

As for facial activity: Daniel readily admits that he likes to play to the audience. At a season-ending pizza party at the Shed, he was named cowinner of the company's annual Empty Box award, for over-acting. In act 2, just before his comrades perform their gulling, he gives a soliloquy that expresses

Benedick's attitudes toward women and marriage. At one point he makes a list of womanly virtues and claims indifference to every one of them.

> One woman is fair, yet I am well. Another is wise, yet I am well. Another virtuous, yet I am well. But till all graces be in one woman, one woman shall not come in my grace.

At "One woman is fair," Daniel scanned the audience and gestured toward a pretty woman sitting in her seat. At "Another is wise" he scanned again, indicating a woman on the other side of the house. At "Another is virtuous" he scanned one way, then the other . . . and finally continued his speech, having despaired of finding a virtuous woman he could point to. This bit always drew an appreciative laugh. The audience, Daniel knew, loves to be made part of the show.

Another example: Benedick's gulling scene begins with the song "Sigh No More," sung by the self-deprecating Balthasar, who warns that no note of his is worth the noting. While Leonato, Claudio, and Don Pedro look on, Benedick hides (at least he thinks he is hiding) behind the stage-right sittable, writhing in pain at the horrid singing and the song's stupid sentiment. When the song ends, Don Pedro says:

> **Don Pedro:** By my troth, a good song.
> **Balthasar:** And an ill singer, my lord.

Don Pedro: Ha, no, no, faith. Thou singest well enough for a shift.

Benedick [aside]: An he had been a dog that should have howled thus, they would have hanged him; and I pray God his bad voice bode no mischief . . .

Of course there's no musical notation in the Folio text. In APT's version the song was set to music written by John Tanner, who had Claudio, Leonato, and Don Pedro joining Balthasar to create a lovely four-part harmony. At first Frank thought it was too lovely and asked Tanner to change it. But in the end they kept the song as it was and used it as part of Benedick's torment. The prettier they sing the more it drives him crazy.

This necessitated a change in the text. Because all four men were singing now, Benedick's reference to "his bad voice" had to be changed to "their bad voices." Frank asked Daniel to make the change one day in rehearsal. Daniel replied almost instantly, as though he'd been waiting for this opening:

"I'll give you a *their*, David, if you'll give me a *you*." He wanted to change "they would have hanged him" to "you would have hanged him."

"I'll take it to the audience," Daniel said. He knew they would probably applaud at the end of the song. Instead of muttering to himself as other Benedicks had done, he would look out at the theatergoers and complain directly to them: *What are you clapping for? If a dog had made those noises you would have hanged him.*

"I'm an actor," he told me. "I will do what makes people happy. And I will do what I'm good at. And sometimes those two things are not what the play needs." He was not surprised or dismayed when he heard the director's note about his overactive face. A few days later he was laughing about it. "I've got Evelyn going, do you know you added 43 seconds to that monologue? You know what that is? That's you making some facial activity."

No one wanted or expected Daniel to keep his pliable face or his audience-pleasing instincts under wraps, especially not during the gulling scene. Its purpose is to be funny. But he had to balance the clownish Benedick with the wounded soldier he would present in the love scene, and the fearful but gallant suitor who would leave Beatrice saying, "As you hear of me, so think of me." He was grateful for the reminder. "Once you say this is the track we're going to be on, you need people keeping you on the right track."

DOUBT

———

The "slow" that David Frank was always warning about—the thing that happens when the audience knows what's coming—is not easy to avoid in the case of a 400-year-old classic. Everyone in the theater knows that Beatrice and Benedick are going to end up together. That's what happens in Shakespeare comedies. (That's what happens in Hollywood comedies.) So how do you make the audience forget? How do you keep them guessing? This question was ever-present in the rehearsal room as Frank and the actors worked. From one end of a line to the other, from the beginning of a speech to the end, from prelude to curtain they sought surprise at every opportunity.

By 5.2, the audience and most of the characters know that Don John's plot has failed. Borachio (whose name means drunkard) has overserved himself and boasted to a buddy about playacting with Margaret in Hero's bedroom window. The deputy constables of the Watch, overhearing this confession, have arrested him, and his sponsor Don John has fled from Messina.

(Note that it's the bumbling bumpkins who end up saving the aristocrats from the consequences of their grasping and duplicity.)

But Beatrice and Benedick don't know any of this. They still think that Hero's honor needs to be defended and avenged. Benedick tells Beatrice that he has challenged Claudio, and with this news her heart melts. For the first time they put down their verbal weapons and speak dreamily, without sarcasm or irony, joking and laughing as lovers do.

> **Benedick:** I pray thee now tell me, for which of my bad parts didst thou first fall in love with me?
> **Beatrice:** For them all together, which maintain so politic a state of evil that they will not admit any good part to intermingle with them. But for which of my good parts did you first suffer love for me?
> **Benedick:** Suffer love—a good epithet. I do suffer love indeed, for I love thee against my will.
> **Beatrice:** In spite of your heart, I think. Alas, poor heart. If you spite it for my sake I will spite it for yours, for I will never love that which my friend hates.

Benedick: Thou and I are too wise to woo
peaceably. . . .
And now tell me, how doth your cousin?
Beatrice: Very ill.
Benedick: And how do you?
Beatrice: Very ill too.
Benedick: Serve God, love me, and mend.

The mood has changed from jokey to tender. Are they about to seal it with a kiss?

Shakespeare doesn't say. The moment is interrupted by Ursula, Hero's gentlewoman, who comes on in aflutter:

Madam, you must come to your uncle. Yonder's old coil at home. It is proved my Lady Hero hath been falsely accused, the Prince and Claudio mightily abused, and Don John is the author of all, who is fled and gone. Will you come presently?

In a filmed version of the New York Shakespeare Festival's 1972 production, Beatrice and Benedick share a long kiss before Ursula barges in. In other versions they kiss even before this scene. But Frank didn't want any kissing just yet. "For 40 years—no, 50 years!—I've been telling myself, don't tell the story before you get there. Don't give up any more than you have to." He wanted to keep the audience in suspense as long as possible. In the end, Colleen

Madden showed him how, inventing a gambit that held the tension almost until the final moment.

In the last scene, the young lovers Claudio and Hero are reunited. He thought she was dead (never having seen a Shakespeare comedy) but now learns that she's not. And, she swears to him again, she is a maid. Never mind that he shamed and slandered her and stalked off thinking her a corpse—he's a handsome soldier. All's forgiven! "To the chapel," cries the friar, and everyone heads off for the wedding.

But wait, Benedick says. He means to make it a double wedding. He asks Beatrice, "Do not you love me?" Beatrice answers "Why no, no more than reason." Whereupon Benedick refers to the testimony he heard while he was hiding in the trees:

> **Benedick:** Why then, your uncle and the Prince and Claudio
> Have been deceived. They swore you did.
> **Beatrice:** Do not you love me?
> **Benedick:** Troth no, no more than reason.
> **Beatrice:** Why then, my cousin, Margaret, and Ursula
> Are much deceived, for they did swear you did.
> **Benedick:** They swore that you were almost sick for me.
> **Beatrice:** They swore that you were wellnigh dead for me.

Benedick: 'Tis no such matter. Then you do not love me?

Beatrice: No, truly, but in friendly recompense.

It's a scene to puzzle over. What's Benedick getting at with his question? Is this his idea of a proposal? Why does Beatrice answer "no more than reason"? Is she angry, fearful, or just performing for the onlookers as is her habit? There are many ways to play it. In Kenneth Branagh's version, Beatrice is embarrassed by Benedick's question and they spat, the onlookers laughing at their every jape. In Joss Whedon's film, Benedick is hesitant and Beatrice is disgusted by his inconstancy; as she says in the beginning of the play, she knows it of old.

Madden, Daniel, and Frank were still working on this scene in the fourth week of rehearsal. One afternoon, after they had been wrestling with it for about half an hour, Madden asked, "Can we try something for kicks and giggles?" What if the scene were about lightbulbs going on—Beatrice and Benedick each realizing that they have been gulled? Madden thought she'd seen it done that way in some other production, but it was new to Frank and Daniel (and eventually Madden doubted her recollection). I've not seen it done her way in at least five filmed versions, but I think her interpretation is strongly suggested by the parallelism in Beatrice's and Benedick's lines. In any case, here's how they wound up playing it:

> **Benedick** (grandly and publicly, showing off for the crowd): Do not you love me?
> **Beatrice** (smiling shyly, placing her hand in his, then delivering a playful jab): Why no, no more than reason.
> **Benedick** (going along with her joke): Why then, your uncle and the Prince and Claudio
> Have been deceived. They swore you did.
> **Beatrice** (still having fun): Do not you love me?
> **Benedick** (getting her back playfully): Troth no, no more than reason.
> **Beatrice:** Why then, my cousin, Margaret, and Ursula
> Are much deceived, for they did . . .

She hesitates as she hears herself repeating Benedick's words almost verbatim. A light goes on in her head; she finishes the line quietly, flustered, just now realizing what has happened.

> . . . swear *you* did.

Benedick's eyes widen; the realization crosses his face. But it can't be! He blurts hopefully:

> **Benedick:** They swore you were almost sick for me.

Now it's confirmed in Beatrice's mind; she presents her evidence:

Beatrice: They swore you were wellnigh dead for me.

They've been duped! Benedick crumples with disappointment.

Benedick: Then (pulling his hand away) you do
not love me?

They're back where they started in act 1. Beatrice turns, shattered, and retreats into self-protection.

Beatrice: No, truly, but in friendly recompense.

Frank lit up. "Oh that's great, that's brilliant, Colleen. Now it's another story: they've suddenly discovered that the entire foundation of their love affair was actually a trick!" What do they do now? With just 40 lines left in the play, Madden had found a way to keep doubt alive.

Of course this is act 5 of a Shakespeare comedy, where no end lies loose for long. The doubt is quickly banished: Look here, Claudio has in his hand a love-wracked sonnet written to Beatrice by Benedick! And, what do you know, Hero has found one to Benedick from Beatrice!

Benedick: A miracle! Here's our own hands
against our hearts. Come, I will have thee, but by
this light, I take thee for pity.
Beatrice: I would not deny you, but by this good
day, I yield upon great persuasion, and partly
to save your life, for I was told you were in a
consumption.
Benedick: Peace, I will stop your mouth.

And there's the kiss.

CURTAIN CALL

———

The last performance of *Much Ado*, and the last of APT's outdoor season, was given on October 5. The temperature was 48 degrees as the show ended, so the "cold plan" was in effect: Bob Morgan had specified what extra layers each actor could wear if necessary. (There are also heat plans that list what garments can be removed; sometimes the plans also involve fans, ice packs, cold towels, and spray bottles.) Evelyn Matten noted that the "delightful" audience of 930 gave a standing ovation.

David Daniel led the cast in their bows. Then he and Colleen Madden took center stage and the applause grew louder. Daniel stood aside, as if gallantly to give the leading lady her moment, then suddenly changed his mind and stepped forward himself. I took it as good-natured self-criticism—

his acknowledgment that he had stolen the show, and partly by dubious means. The audience had been spellbound by his backside declaration of love, and touched by the hurt and confusion of his lonely soldier, but they were more likely to remember his lazzi and facial activity. Madden was and would remain much the better-known actor, one of APT's most important stars. But in his fifteenth year with the company, Daniel had promoted himself from the ranks of lordies and dukies.

It was a good year for him. He gave a captivating performance as a shy and selfless physician in Shaw's *The Doctor's Dilemma*; and five days after *Much Ado* closed, he began previews for his third show of the season, *Alcestis*, a seldom-seen play by Euripides translated by the British poet Ted Hughes. Again, David Frank was directing. Daniel played both Apollo and Heracles, the latter as a hard-partying rock 'n' roll mythic hero in a leather jacket, a red bandana headband, and a Fu Manchu mustache— another high-profile role. The *Isthmus* critic Amelia Cook Fontella called his performance "completely unforgettable."

Bob Morgan was the designer who dressed Daniel for that show. The disappointments of *Much Ado* long forgotten, Morgan not only collaborated with Frank on *Alcestis* but also signed up to do another show with him the following year.

The play sold 22,671 tickets, about 73 percent of

capacity, which counts as a solid success in APT's scheme of things. Ticket revenue was more than $750,000, a little better than projected. *Much Ado* was the best seller of the season but not the top earner: *Earnest* was so well received that a performance was added after the start of the season. It sold almost as many tickets as *Much Ado* in four fewer performances, and its per-ticket yield was higher because fewer of its sales were to deep-discount student groups.

I thought the last show was clearer than I had seen it before. Not that it ever was unclear to me (how could it be? I'd sat in on rehearsals and knew the actors' intent at every turn), but the meanings seemed sharper and better defined. At the same time the performance seemed to move faster. I later checked Matten's stopwatch record, expecting to see that a few minutes' running time had been shaved off, but the speed turned out to be an illusion. Matten was not surprised. "We opened in June, we closed October 5, that's five months. If you say the same words or you think about the same words two or three times a week, you will get more facile with them. The ideas will become clearer. The things that we were working really hard on as you watched us in June, getting the images and the pictures and the clarity of thought, now they are like, well, duh! So I think that familiarity of the actors, that comfort in their mouth, will come across as less labored—it would seem lighter and come quicker. It rolls differently."

I watched closely on the last night to see what Colleen Madden was doing with "Kill Claudio." She said it quickly, after two deep inhales. The audience laughed.

THE END

———

Once Beatrice and Benedick kiss, it's a race to the finish. Benedick forgives himself for all his railing against marriage. "Never flout at me for what I have said against it. For man is a giddy thing, and this is my conclusion." He and Claudio hug and make up. He notices his comrade Don Pedro, the matchmaker, on the sideline. "Prince, thou art sad, get thee a wife, get thee a wife."

A messenger races in with the news that Don John has been apprehended in flight. Benedick calls for dancing and the music begins. As the supporting characters pair off and whirl around the stage, Benedick and Beatrice lock eyes from opposite sides of the garden. The dancers fade into the background (a neat trick by choreographer Linda Fortunato) and the couple comes together center stage, joining in

what David Frank called a "clinch for the ages." No
kiss, nothing sexual, just a deep, satisfied embrace.
They have found each other and they are hanging on
for life. The lights go down and the audience erupts.

ACKNOWLEDGMENTS

The stage is a very public workplace, but the re-hearsal room is intimate—not really a place for outsiders. I will never forget the warmth and generosity with which the cast and staff of *Much Ado* welcomed me in, or their patience as they endured my pestering and ignorance. It was a privilege to be among them and watch them work. I can only hope they see themselves portrayed accurately and fairly here.

Thanks to David Frank, the director of the show and the recently retired head of APT, who swung the door open for me and explained so much of what I saw there. He loves to talk about theater, and Shakespeare in particular, but I suspect he prefers a more knowledgeable interlocutor than he got in me. He was extremely busy during rehearsals, but always cheerful, patient, and uncommonly candid, a rare combination that made my work easy.

The same should be said of the many actors, designers, craftspeople, and company staffers who made time to talk with me or help in other ways big and small. Many are named repeatedly in the text, but I should thank here some who are mentioned only in passing or not at all: Brenda DeVita, James DeVita, Carrie Van Hallgren, Nate Burger, Jeb Burris, Michael Broh, Sara Stellick, Scott Rött, April McKinnis, Jess Amend, Michael Peterson, Eliot Garfield, Bill Paton, Carey Cannon. And Jen Trieloff, APT's much-loved properties director (and an accomplished set designer at other theaters), who gave me more time than he had time for. He died, unexpectedly and way too young, after the 2014 outdoor season was over.

Thanks to Travis Knight, who rekindled a dormant interest in this project; to Brian Mani, Colleen Madden, David Daniel, and Bob Morgan, who went out of their way to make me feel welcome; and to Michele Bindl, Carol Jefferson, Kate LaRocque, Michele Traband, Jessi Veverka, Beth Ferstl, Gayle Wood, and many others who helped me more than they knew just by smiling and saying hello.

Paul Bentzen and Sarah Day, two actors who go back to APT's very early days, spoke with me freely and in detail about the beginnings of the company, which did not play as big a role in my story as I originally expected. That was my fault, not theirs; our conversations provided invaluable background and texture for which I'm very grateful. Thanks also to Sandy Robbins, for a couple of very enlightening interviews; to David Kraemer, Dusty

Priebe, and Anne Occhiogrosso, for filling in some of the ancient history; and to Damien Jaques, for encouragement and the sort of jump-start that only a fellow journalist can provide.

Finally at APT, my most elaborate and humble thanks go to Evelyn Matten and Sara Young. These are two of the most competent people I've ever met, and they gave me a great deal of practical support. But I'm most grateful to them for more kindness and forbearance than I deserved.

On the home front, thanks to Doug Seibold at Agate, a sympathetic publisher and an astute editor, for giving this book a place in the world, and thanks to his colleagues for dressing it up in this attractive package and bringing it to market. Thanks to my good old friends John Conroy, who read the manuscript and offered insightful comments, and Tony Judge, who introduces people. And most of all, thanks to my A-team of readers and supporters, Jack and Rose Lenehan and my wife, Mary Williams, who are always helping to make my story better.

Of course any errors in this book are mine alone and I apologize for them in advance. (There's always something.) I will do my best to present corrections and dissents on my website, michaellenehan.com.

SOURCES

I am not learned, ambitious, or foolish enough to attempt a Shakespeare bibliography, but in case I have succeeded in stirring any reader's curiosity, I'll mention a few sources that I found useful and informative.

When I started on this project, I asked some knowledgeable people if there was anything I could read that would quickly show me the lay of the land—educate me about Shakespeare's life and time, the way he worked, the state of the theater art, the history of the texts. The question seemed to stump everyone I asked, possibly because *The Norton Shakespeare* is so fundamental they assumed I must be looking for something else. But Stephen Greenblatt's long introductory essay was just what I needed, an excellent starting point for any curious reader. And the Norton's play texts are concisely but smartly annotated and footnoted; like any modern reader I encountered many baffling references and antiquated usages, but rarely one that the Norton failed to explain on the same page. This book, all

3,240 pages of it, was constantly at my side as I wrote. Its *Much Ado* section is so well thumbed that I can find it by feel and see it from several feet away. I had the first edition, published in 1997; the third was released in 2015.

I was also informed, impressed, and entertained by Marjorie Garber's very readable *Shakespeare After All* (Pantheon, 2004), a collection of lively essays on each of the 38 plays, developed from Garber's lecture courses at Harvard and Yale. Bernard Beckerman's *Shakespeare at the Globe* (Macmillan, 1962) provided enlightening details on how the plays were produced and what audiences expected from them.

No matter how good your footnotes, or how elucidating your critical essays, reading Shakespeare is hard. Watching Shakespeare is fun, or usually is, or ought to be. No reading experience can compare with seeing and hearing the language brought to life for you by a troupe of talented actors led by an imaginative director. And if you're interested in theater craft and how it applies in the case of an author who's been dead for 400 years, there's no better education than comparing one troupe's version with others. For this we are lucky to have film and video. I was able to see no fewer than five different productions of *Much Ado*, and probably a couple more that I have forgotten.

Two for starters: the 1993 version directed by Kenneth Branagh, with Branagh as Benedick,

Emma Thompson (then his wife) as Beatrice, Denzel Washington as the princely Don Pedro, and Keanu Reeves as the oily villain Don John. The setting, in the words of the *New York Times* critic Vincent Canby, is "a magnificent Tuscan villa in the erotic heat of an Italian summer. The period is not specified, although it seems to be a distant, vaguely Renaissance past." Canby called it a "ravishing entertainment," which is more than I would say, but it is a good introduction to the play for modern audiences.

A vivid and very enlightening contrast is the 2012 version shot in black and white by Joss Whedon, who wrote and directed the *Avengers* movies and created the TV series *Buffy the Vampire Slayer*. This is my favorite film *Much Ado*, a modern-dress version set in a nice house (Whedon's, actually) in Southern California. Shakespeare's original language is preserved, and it works surprisingly well in the contemporary context. A.O. Scott of the *Times* called it (in June of 2013) "perhaps the liveliest and most purely delightful movie I have seen so far this year."

More contrast still can be had in a version by the New York Shakespeare Festival, filmed for TV by CBS and released in 1973. This one is set in the United States in the early 1900s. Sam Waterston is Benedick and Kathleen Widdoes is Beatrice. Direction was by A.J. Antoon and Nick Havinga.

A Globe Theatre version (2012) with Eve Best

ABOUT THE AUTHOR

Michael Lenehan is the former editor and executive editor of the *Chicago Reader* and a former contributing editor of the *Atlantic*. He's the author of the Agate Midway book *Ramblers: Loyola Chicago 1963—The Team that Changed the Color of College Basketball.* He grew up in Fair Lawn, New Jersey, and graduated from the University of Notre Dame. He lives in Chicago with his wife, Mary Williams.